Game Ready

52 Takeaways
for Winning

Foreword by
Phillip Fulmer

Coach Mickey Marley

"Coach Marley's heart-felt stories teach vital lessons on the art of business, coaching, education, leadership, and life in general. These lessons exemplify the qualities of patience, virtue, dedication, courage, camaraderie, team, passion, and the love of sports, which describe Coach Marley, as well as most successful people."

Dan Black, President, TSSAA State Legislative Council

"My first introduction to Mickey Marley was in 1986 at Lambuth University where I was a wide receiver and he was on the coaching staff. The things that stood out the most about Coach Marley were his leadership, dedication, commitment and his heart for people. These attributes have carried him throughout his successful high school coaching career and have become his approach to life. He is a man of faith with strong character that I'm proud to call my friend. I believe you will find this book insightful and inspirational, coming from a man with an intense drive to succeed."

Dan Crockett, President/CEO, Franklin American Mortgage Company

"Coach Marley's book is a must read for all young people with dreams of coaching any sport. In a time where the basics and fundamentals are overlooked far too often, Mickey tells stories and shares experiences that are refreshing, entertaining and useful. Not everything is as complicated as it might seem, and his advice proves to support this. With someone with as much experience, knowledge and success as Coach, we can all stand to gain a few nuggets of wisdom."

Thomas McDaniel, Head Coach Christian Brothers High School: President, Tennessee Football Coaches Association

"Coach Marley does a great job of sharing his wealth of knowledge in this book. Being a four-year starter at the University of Tennessee and a high school coach, I have been around great coaches. I believe this book does the difficult job of taking complex ideas and simplifying them for the masses. This is a must read for coaches and players wanting to know how to develop a winning football program."

James Wilhoit, Professional Football Kicking Coach, Brentwood Academy, Brentwood, Tennessee

"As the owner and CEO of a company since 1987, I quickly realized that in order for our company to succeed and be successful, then we had to develop a team atmosphere. An atmosphere that encouraged individual effort while recognizing that we were interdependent on all our team members to achieve success. In order for success to be achieved, a team needs leadership from its members, which starts with a coach. This book relays some very thoughtful practical concepts and observations a leader should possess."

Mike McWherter, President,Central Distributors, Jackson, Tennessee

"This book is filled with practical knowledge and advice regarding leadership. It comes from a football background but is applicable in all areas of life. Mickey has always been a leader. These principals will guide and inspire you to be a better person and achieve more in life. I highly recommend this book."

Steve Gaines, PhD, Senior Pastor, Bellevue Baptist Church, Memphis, Tennessee; President, Southern Baptist Convention

"Mickey Marley's book is an interesting read. I found his 'Takeaways' to be thought provoking and very applicable to both my coaching career and my life."

Steve Stripling, Assistant Coach, University of Cincinnati

"Coach Marley's book is a great read for all walks of life. His awareness of having a positive winning attitude combined with hard work is a common theme. He is very transparent. Many powerful quotes are contained in his book. Anyone wanting to advance their career or excel in excellence should read this book."

Gary A. Taylor, businessman

"I've had the privilege of knowing Coach Marley over twenty years. I witnessed the transformation of a man who knew a lot about football to a man who knows a lot about life. His book details the lessons he's learned from a three-dimensional perspective, addressing the physical, mental, and spiritual. His heart is to challenge every coach and athlete to pursue excellence for the Glory of the master coach Jesus Christ."

Michael Sparks, FCA, West Tennessee Director, 1983-2012, Fellowship Bible Church Men's Pastor

"Solid reading…This easy read is a compendium of years of outstanding coaching and mentoring experience. Coach Marley's 'Takeaways' are a clear and concise guided missile for success, not just in sports but in any endeavor."

Robert Fay, retired NBC Executive

In honor of my mama, **Mary Margaret Marley**, a true treasure to me and my brothers. Her influence on my life has been profound. She always encouraged me to be the very best I could be at whatever I did. Mama always made me feel as though I could accomplish anything, and that is a true gift I will cherish forever.

Out of her genuine love for others she gave of herself. She truly has a sweet uplifting spirit that is a blessing from God. I dedicate this book to the greatest influence in my life, Mama.

Contents

Foreword

Winning is anything but easy. Whether you're playing a game of football or vying for thirty minutes of time with a business prospect, the priority is always to play to win.

I have known many players and coaches throughout my life. They all want the same thing—victory. But wanting it is only half the battle. You must set out to learn from every experience, on and off the field. It can be a thankless job sometimes. Each new day presents the unexpected for all of us, whether we're coaching young athletes or directing a team in the workplace. Some people embrace the challenge ahead of them, while others decide it's easier to go back to bed.

Like intense competition on the football field, the pressure of life can test you. If you're prepared mentally, physically and emotionally, chances are you will come out on the other side, but not without some bruises. Coaches and players, especially these days, need authenticity and wisdom. Only a seasoned leader, one who not only cares about an athlete's success for what it can bring to the team, but what it can mean for them personally, can offer this kind of playbook.

Coach Mickey Marley is one of those highly focused individuals who chose to build on his strengths and weaknesses, the good experiences and the bad ones. Now, he's in the best position of anyone I know in the football coaching world to share his knowledge with people who are determined to get up every day and meet the known and the unknown challenge before them.

Mickey's book is a darn good read and will strike a chord intellectually as it pulls at the heart strings. Coaches, young or old, business people, teachers, parents, and folks from any walk of life will enjoy Mickey's straight forward, witty, and motivating stories gained from his thirty-seven years as a very successful football coach.

He shares his passion for the game, his love for his kids and lessons for life that we can all gain from.

Phillip Fulmer, Director of Athletics, University of Tennessee
Head Football Coach, 1993-2008
March 2018

Introduction

I have been blessed by God to live what I think is a unique, great life. My three brothers and I were brought up to be mentally, physically and emotionally tough, but not in a bully type fashion. We were to do what we were told, when we were told. We were also to be polite, kind, and courteous to all people. Sounds good, and it was good.

Now, the flip side to the story was we were also brought up not to cause trouble; but when trouble got started, we were not to back down. We were also brought up to look out for one another. My daddy told us all once that if he ever heard about one of us turning on another he would whip our you know what. Well, he didn't have to because we did, and still do, look out for one another.

My daddy was a real-life cowboy. He ran horse and cattle operations all across the country. Mama was a cowboy's wife and raised four boys into what I think are four fine men. When I came along my family lived where my daddy's horse and cattle operations were in Tennessee. Puryear, Gleason, Bolivar and eventually Franklin. Franklin, Tennessee is where Mama called home. Her people basically migrated there during the Civil War era and stayed. We lived in Williamson County, actually, in a little place called Kingfield. We would go through Leiper's Fork almost every day. That's when Puckett's Grocery was actually a grocery.

I learned a lot about work ethic on those ranches. We broke horses, worked and branded cattle, hauled hay, dug post holes and put up barbed wire fence. You name it, we did it. Now, I always loved sports. So naturally my brothers and I did some rodeoing like Daddy. I could ride a horse like nobody's business. In fact, I rode a little bit with some trick riders around some rodeo arenas when daddy was rodeoing. My brothers took to the rodeoing more than I did. I loved playing football, baseball and wrestling. I was fortunate enough to do all three sports in high school. I also had college opportunities in all three sports. I chose football and played four years at the University of Tennessee at Martin. Actually, football coaches were some of the most influential people in my life. My head high school football coach at Franklin High School was Ray Dalton. Coach Dalton got me an opportunity to walk-on at UT Martin. I wound up getting a scholarship and becoming a tri-captain my senior year.

If it hadn't of been for Coach Dalton, I don't know where I would be right now. George MacIntyre was my head football coach at UT Martin. He believed in me enough to give me a chance, and for that I am forever grateful. Coach Fred Pickard was our defensive coordinator. He is a great man. He instilled the physical, mental, and emotional toughness required in the game of football, so that all of us, as players on the defensive side of the ball, felt prepared to compete.

I graduated from UT Martin with a degree in communications. To be honest, if you ask me, 'Why communications?' The answer is, 'I don't know why.' So, I gravitated to what I had always loved - football. I became a graduate assistant football coach at UT Martin in 1980, and coached defensive backs there until we all got fired in 1985.

In 1986, I was hired as defensive coordinator at Old Hickory Academy in Jackson, Tennessee by one of the greatest men I have ever met, Coach Walter Kilzer. Now, Old Hickory Academy eventually merged with Episcopal Day School in Jackson and the result was University School of Jackson. I became the head football coach of USJ in 1989 and had twenty-seven great years of coaching with some of the best football coaches and players anywhere.

We went to five state championship games; ten semi-final games and a bunch of quarter final games. Most importantly, the players I had the great opportunity to coach were outstanding young men of character and courage. They loved playing football. We prided ourselves on being mentally, physically, and emotionally tough. *You achieve nothing great on your own.* It was the assistant coaches that

I had the great privilege to work with that were the very backbone of our team and to all of them I am eternally grateful.

As with everything in life all things come to an end and my coaching career ended at University School of Jackson in 2015 after a semi-final season. I was out of coaching for one season before returning in 2017 to coach at Trenton Rosenwald Middle School in Trenton, Tennessee. Remember how I told you that Coach Walter Kilzer was one of the greatest men I ever met? Well, I am about to tell you what makes life great, the irony of events in our lives makes life great. Coach Kilzer was from Trenton and coached at Trenton Peabody High School for thirty years. In fact, the stadium is named after him. So, I am coaching at the latter part of my career at Walter Kilzer Stadium! Oh, and let me throw this in - Coach Kilzer was 'best man' at my wedding when I married the love of my life, Lisa. Now, how is that for ironic!

Lisa and I have two beautiful daughters, Jordan and Kristen, a great son-in-law, J.P. Harrison, and three awesome grandsons—Jack, Eli and Charlie Harrison. Don't you know we have fun playing whatever sport is in season in the backyard. Being a granddad is awesome! I have also been fortunate enough to have been inducted into sports hall of fames in three different institutions. In 2012, I was named to the Jackson/Madison County Hall of Fame. In 2016, I was inducted into the Franklin High School Athletic Hall of Fame and that same year I was honored to be inducted into the Tennessee Football Coaches Association Hall of Fame.

Again, only through the collective work of many outstanding people in my life was I able to become worthy of these honors. I have always believed you have to 'surround yourself with great people' to become successful. I have truly been blessed in this area of my life.

You may now be asking yourself why, 'Coach, why did you write this book?' Well, I am gonna tell you. First of all, the things covered in this book are straight forward and to the point, like me. Also, the words are my words so there will be a lot of *ain'ts* and *cain'ts*. The topics covered are really things I know to be true. I believe each one of these pages contains elements of a play book for life. I wrote them to give to others what has been given to me – what I call *really pretty simple insight*. I know by reading this book you will have a chance to be successful in anything you set out to do - be it in football, in business, or, most importantly, in life, **in living every day of life.**

Through my many years of coaching, I have often wondered about and or done the things that I cover in this book. To be quite honest, I truly believe more straightforward, *honest* talking is the way to go. Now to add to that, we have to do more doing than talking to get anything accomplished. I believe a person must possess pride, discipline, courage, outstanding work ethic and be selfless *not selfish* to succeed in whatever endeavor they undertake.

It's really pretty simple. This book is written in a plain ol' fashion style and about topics that will help you and your team grow and improve. That's about as simple as I can make it for now. So, enjoy, and let's get to reading!

Desire To Play

Growing up can be the hardest work we ever do. Time, place and people are not coincidental to our story. Coach Marley treasures his childhood because of the poignant lessons he learned from family.

I vividly remember living out in the rural Kingfield community, past Hillsboro and back in Waddell Hollow. It was my sophomore year of high school. Daddy had just moved us from West Tennessee, where he had been working between Bolivar and Middleton on a horse and cattle operation. He took on a new job at a farm in Franklin, but our family lived about 15 miles out of town.

I was supposed to go to Hillsboro School, but there was one slight problem. Hillsboro didn't have a football team. Now, my two older brothers, Bill and Joe, had graduated from Franklin High School. Bill was in the band. Joe played football. Both went on to MTSU pursuing those talents on the college level.

Mama knew I wanted to play football, wrestle and play baseball, so she drove me past Hillsboro to Franklin High, along with my younger brother Cody who attended Franklin Elementary. That was not a small commitment.

I didn't drive a car to school like some other kids because we only had one car and that was Mama's. She sure put in a lot of miles back and forth to practices and games. My grandparents lived in Franklin, so a lot of times I would stay with them on school nights.

Eventually, we moved from Kingfield to Clovercroft Road, then to an apartment my grandmother had in the back of her place, then to Adam's Street before returning to grandmother's apartment. You are probably saying that's a lot of moves and you are right! There was one thing that was always a constant and that was Mama always wanted what was best for her boys.

It all worked out well for us. I went to UT-Martin, played four years of college football, graduated and started coaching as a graduate assistant there in 1980. Bill, Joe and Cody all went to college at

MTSU and graduated. Bill and Joe both have had great careers in education in Franklin and Williamson County. Cody went on to become a stand-up comedian, comedy writer, rodeo announcer and buyer and seller of musical instruments on the internet.

Circumstances don't prevent you from accomplishing your dreams when you are persistent. But you must have help along the way from someone who believes in you even though you may not believe in yourself. That someone for me, and my brothers, remains the constant in all our lives. She is Mary Margaret Marley, otherwise known as Mama!

Takeaway #1
There Ain't No Cain't

Thirty-seven years of coaching football taught me one very important lesson. To be a true champion, a true winner in any arena, there is no room for the words *cain't, cannot,* or *will not.* **These are non-existent in the vocabulary of a true winner**. You must decide you are a person who **can** in all circumstances. Those circumstances will vary from person to person and team to team, but the basic choices really do not.

Trust me, I know just how capable people are when it comes to learning all sorts of lessons and applying that knowledge every day. My coaching career gave me some great insight into how players learn. To be able to watch young kids improve as people and players is a gift. I have felt nothing less than satisfaction every season I have stepped onto the field.

Yes, I have experienced winning seasons, but I've also had disappointments. **In both situations, attitude was everything.** I have witnessed the heartache and disappointment that comes when one of the kids I was coaching got injured - not for myself, but for the player. He is the one who has been injured playing the game he loves. In one singular moment, doubt arrives and begins to work on his psyche.

We are all impacted every day by unexpected, undesirable events. In those moments, the player and the coach must respond. The response is more than just motioning for a trainer, but is the beginning of choice.

The champion and winner that we all really want to be and, by the way, were created to be can only rely on a response of *I can*. Sure, the negative does exist. There is no way around that fact. Yet, the power is believing that there are plenty of available tools within you that are available if you decide to turn on the positive and let the negative sit quietly in the background.

Remember this statement. ***Cain't is not sustainable, but can is attainable.***

A winner is always trying to increase their ability to learn new abilities every day. You will fail if you do not understand how to tap into your entire set of abilities. These are the tools you have been given but are still learning to use. For instance, your first shot at using a hammer may be mediocre, but the story does not end there. Settling for mediocre or average is a choice. If the hammer is not getting the job done, you probably need a new tool. But if you have a cain't attitude, the outcome will be pretty obvious. ***The choice of average or great is not a roll of the dice or a place where you are born, it is a choice you must make.***

So, if positive thoughts and actions direct someone who wants each day to be a winning day or each game to be a winning game, the task ahead will be more like play than work. Ultimately, the result is a lifetime of winning and gaining, not losing. Your life will begin to resemble, the life of someone who wants to be a champion, not only for his or her own sake, but also for the sake of others.

It's really pretty simple. A positive 'can do attitude' beats a 'cain't attitude' every time. A positive attitude is infectious; a 'cain't attitude' will ultimately kill you. There ain't no cain't when it comes to winning.

Takeaway #2
Altering the Self-Esteem Syndrome

There is no question that a team is made up of individuals all trying to accomplish a common goal. It stands to reason that a player will perform better, accomplish more and have a better chance of success if he feels good about himself and what he is doing. *Helping your player achieve a level of confidence through skill improvement is a critical objective for every coach*.

If you think about it, we as coaches all face the same dilemma. Do you tell them what they need to hear or do you tell them what they want to hear? Truth is you must tell them what they need to hear as honestly and directly as possible. To do anything less is simply to falsely inflate a player's ego, which does nothing to build skill-based confidence. *Giving out false self-esteem doesn't do anyone any favors, except your opponent.* A world where everyone gets a participation trophy, certificate or ribbon does not exist in the real world of competition. Telling a player up front when he needs to make corrections prevents problems down the road for the entire team. Blunt assessment and honest critique matters most. What is at stake here, quite frankly, is the success or failure of the team.

Don't get me wrong, I believe a player's self-esteem is important, but it must be developed legitimately. Coaches determine where the opportunity exists within each player. The best way to do that is through an honest individual player assessment. Every coach has his or her own style, which is as it should be. If that style is *'firm but fair,'* then demonstrate that every time. If that style is *'relaxed but always in control,'* then consistently deliver that style. But never confuse players by sugarcoating what needs to be fixed, no matter what kind of coaching style you use.

The job of building true self-esteem in an individual player is predicated on a coach taking time to show that player how to improve and holding him accountable for improving. When you get that you get a better, more confident player and, most importantly, a more confident individual. The more of those you get, the better your team gets. I call that **Team Esteem**.

There is nothing more satisfying than to coach a team that is confident, not cocky, but confident. It stands to reason these players will have a chance to dominate every time they compete if they follow the game plan and feed off the **Team Esteem** that has been created.

These statements sum up the job ahead when it comes to building **Team Esteem.**

- You as a coach determine the self-esteem syndrome.
- In the real world of competition everyone does not receive a trophy.
- Coach with a consistent style that never falls back on the temptation to sugarcoat.
- Turn individual self-esteem into **Team Esteem**.
- Watch as individual and **Team Esteem** combine to create true confidence.

It's really very simple. Giving out false self-esteem doesn't do anyone any favors, except your opponent.

Takeaway #3
Change or Get Changed

Change is inevitable. It's just a fact of life and always has been. Like it or not, things change in ways that are well beyond your control as players and coaches. I have found that change is not the challenge, as much as how I choose to react to it. I offer you a couple of questions to consider with your team.

1. Are we going to be the game changer?
2. Are we going to let someone or some event be the game changer?

Those two questions present themselves every day. You can act intentionally with purpose and clarity or you can sit back and watch, basically be the observer of another's actions. It's your choice. Either way, you will be impacted.

First, take a look at the role of the game changer coach. Be it Little League or the NFL, the decision to pursue the game changer approach builds on the same core strategies. Coaching the game of football, including schematics, teaching drills, utilizing technology and promoting player development, is an ever-changing proposition. To be successful, which means setting out to create a championship caliber team, you must coach to your players' best abilities.

If that sounds like common sense, hold that thought. You would be surprised how many coaches try to put a round peg in a square hole. Imagine being the new coach in town and the first temptation is to implement a system of offense and defense that reflects your past achievements but does not begin to consider the abilities of your players, let alone attempt to adapt to their strengths.

More specifically, a new head coach enters a high school program and immediately shifts the offense from the "I-formation" that is best suited for the players to a "Spread," throw-it-around, sprinkle in some run team or vice-versa.

In contrast, consider the coach who has been with the same high school football program for several years. His mantra is to keep doing the same thing year after year because that's the way he's always done it. If that means success for the coach great, but if the players' abilities and skill levels change every season and the coach doesn't adapt to his new personnel, that is not so great.

Adjust, adapt and overcome with the team and situation at hand. That requires a coach to see the big picture, but also to always look down the road for cues signaling when change needs to be implemented. If a tire is leaking air, and the driver is doing nothing about it, eventually that driver will be dealing with a flat. As a football coach, you are hired to coach the team. If you allow too many flats to occur you may literally find yourself fixing flats for a living.

Should you choose to let someone else be the game changer, be mindful.

I have never understood why a coach or a player would let someone else be the determinant. Again, we all have different situations and circumstances. But the key is how you, the coach, responds. It is your duty to prepare your team and all those involved, including parents, to the very best of your ability. Regardless of the caliber of competition on the schedule, it is your job to get your team as physically, mentally and emotionally ready as possible.

A win is never guaranteed, but losing is inevitable without that preparation. My preference is to go down the path of a game changer, one that is worn down from repetitive drills and constant coordination between the head coach and coaching staff. You and your staff are the **determinant** of how your team prepares each week. I can not emphasize enough that you must give all involved what the game of football deserves – the very best of your efforts every day for as long as you coach.

It's really pretty simple. The challenge and objective is to be the game changer or you will eventually get changed.

Takeaway #4
You Gotta Be You

If it is not already clear, let me underscore at this point that the words and ideas shared within this book are my own thoughts and opinions gained from thirty-seven years of coaching young people. Fortunately, I have been able to stay connected with many of my players well beyond their seasons of high school football. There is one takeaway I've gained I believe is often overlooked. Being real is required of every member of a team, including the coaches.

I will take that a step further by posing this question: **Why would you want to be someone else when you are already you?**

That may sound like a crazy way to phrase a question but it is always troubling to me when I see a person trying to be someone other than who he or she is. Don't misunderstand me. I am not discouraging players and coaches to have role models, mentors, or hold people they admire up for inspiration in the game.

In life, you have to be yourself. In fact, if you are still unclear about what I mean, look into a mirror at the reflection. No one, but you will ever be there. **You gotta be you.**

Coaches, your football players know instantly when you are attempting to be someone you are not. If trust is the most important aspect of the player-coach relationship, and I believe it is, then it would be foolish to even risk losing that player's trust by trying to be something you are not. They will spot it every time. Let them evaluate you as you are so they are certain of you. Erratic and inconsistent behavior is unsettling and confusing to a player. Consistency is essential to any coaching style.

Without hesitation, be the "old school coach" *if* that is who you are. The term "old school" is offensive to me when I hear it used as a put down by someone trying to discredit a coach. Look for more on that subject as you read further.

Moreover, *if* you are the "players coach" then by all means be that coach. That term is one I also take issue with when it is inaccurately used to describe someone perceived to be soft or undisciplined in their coaching.

Most importantly, *if* you are to maintain trust and credibility with your team, it is vital that you are consistent in your own behavior and attitude every day.

It's really pretty simple. Don't be who you ain't. Be who you are.

Takeaway #5
You're Always Where You're At

Straightforward and direct might be one way to describe who I am. This communication style has served me well for many coaching seasons. The statement *'you're always where you're at'* is one I like to share with players and coaches. Questions about its meaning seem pointless because it speaks for itself. However, don't confuse **'you're always where you're at'** with **'you'll always stay where you're at.'**

Too many people gripe and complain about where they are in life, whether it is their job, family, relationships, team, or fellow players. It seems to me instead of griping and complaining about the situation at hand, there should be a commitment to do something about the situation. Be a problem solver instead of a problem instigator. Be a winner not a whiner.

Your situation - temporary because everything in life is temporary - is yours to handle, be it good or bad. You're always going to be somewhere in life, so make that somewhere as positive and productive as you can. We all have this recurring challenge, but it will always be up to you to position yourself for a gain instead of a loss. A positive attitude is essential and will help with the realization that **'you're always where you're at.'**

When I was in my early days of coaching football, I would sometimes look at the team and say to myself, *'Man, is this all we got?'* I learned pretty quickly, not only was that the wrong way to look at things, but it was counterproductive to boot! I imagine my players back then were looking at me thinking *'Man, is that all we got?'*

Take a minute before you start your day to remind yourself where you are. Step away for a minute and focus on a few words that are positive about how you will approach the hours ahead. ***Once you decide to be positive and productive you won't be tempted*** *quite as easily to whine and complain*. The truth is nobody wants to hear that anyway.

It's really pretty simple. Move from the problem to the solution because the reality is you are always where you're at. But it is your choice to stay.

Takeaway #6
Always Look Around to See What Can Hurt You

My daddy was a real life, legitimate cowboy. In my mind's eye, I remember him being like a character straight from the Old West back in the 1800s. From a young age growing up in Texas, he competed in every rodeo event he could. These competitions were set in some of the most sought-after arenas in the world. From the Pendleton Roundup to the Cheyenne Rodeo to Madison Square Garden, my daddy was there. I even remember once watching him on television when he was featured on ABC's *Wide World of Sports*. In those days, this show was broadcast to millions of viewers at a time when cable preprogrammed channels were non-existent.

Even as an older adult, he continued to compete in team roping events at different events throughout the country. When he wasn't on the rodeo circuit, he oversaw the horse and cattle operations on farms near and far from our home in Williamson County. Eventually, he became a Franklin policeman, joining the small-town force by establishing the department's first modern mounted patrol. My father was Ray 'Kid' Marley.

When I worked with him on one of the cattle operations, he always gave me straight-forward direction. Whether we were working side by side in a barn, out in the round pen breaking horses, or working cattle, he would often say to me, *'Always look around to see what can hurt you!'*

I wasn't much more than five when he first instructed me. I don't know why, but his words didn't scare me. Somehow, I understood what he was telling me and his message has served me well all my life.

He made me keenly aware that I had to know my surroundings. When you are in a corral with a bunch of cattle or horses you become aware real quick. If you don't want to get hurt, become aware of your surroundings.

As a football player and later as a coach, Ray 'Kid' Marley's words have become increasingly important. I took his advice, '**Always look around to see what can hurt you,**' from the barn and field to the gridiron. In football terms, I see it as a warning to become aware of what your opponent can do to hurt you and then prepare for it!

Keep your eyes wide open and be proactive. You will avoid a lot of bad situations. Seems to me most people go through life with their eyes shut and they can't see what can hurt them. Later, they don't understand how what happened exactly happened. They often say they never saw it coming. They had their eyes shut.

As my daddy said, **'Look around.'** The first move is to observe, evaluate and keep your eyes open to see what can hurt you. Physically, you can always get hurt if you don't keep an eye out for what is around you. Physical injury is only the beginning. Adults living with their eyes shut are prone to getting hurt in many ways with long-lasting implications - mental, emotional, financial, and professional.

All I know is at five years old I understood what Kid Marley meant when he spoke those words. Today, I try to use his advice in my own life. It has staying power. Of course, there is no guarantee against getting hurt at some point in life, but I believe his principal sure will reduce the chances! **Always look around to see what can hurt you.**

It's really pretty simple. Take my dad's advice and you'll avoid a lot of potential problems. 'Always look around to see what can hurt you.'

Takeaway #7
If It Ain't Broke...

You've probably heard the saying *'If it ain't broke, don't fix it.'* It may just be me, but I don't understand why people are driven to change what is obviously working well. Let me assure you before I go any further, without question, anything can be improved over time. Human beings will always innovate, always tinker, and always upgrade to new technology when it suits their needs.

I do believe change is great when, and if, it is truly necessary. **What is not so great is change for the sake of change.** You may be thinking, *'No kidding, everybody knows that.'* My reply to your assessment is *'no kidding, everyone doesn't know that.'* You would be surprised how many football coaches I have seen make changes in their football programs just for the sake of change. Whether it be the total team schematics, game schematics or an off-season program, they change the very things that made the team and their coaching successful in the first place.

The common misconception is that what one coach does at his program may not work at another program. If that technique is working for that coach with his players then he's got to stick with it. For the players learning from a new coach, who is bringing in a tried and true program, there will most definitely be adjustment. However, the coach needs to press on and execute the program that has made him successful. *'**If it ain't broke, don't fix it - and I mean don't!'***

If you want to cause yourself a lot of headaches and problems go ahead and try to fix what ain't broke. Coaches sometimes assume they can adopt a team's program and then easily return to their original program. I disagree with that theory of *'**I can always go back to what I was doing before.'*** Without meaning to a coach could wind up like **Humpty Dumpty**, not being able to put that program back together again. **If you have a good thing going, keep doing what you're doing.**

It's really pretty simple. We can all be tempted to fix what isn't broken. Don't fall into that trap. You might just *Humpty Dumpty* your entire program and yourself to boot!

Takeaway #8
Old School, New School, No School

Question: Is there a place for *'old school'* style when it comes to coaching football players today?
Answer: Yes.

Question: Is there a place for *'new school'* style when it comes to coaching football players today?
Answer: Yes

This is an area I've spent countless hours thinking about, and here's why. I was always led to believe 'old school' coaching meant training, teaching, and playing with rough and tough mental and physical exertion. In my experience, 'old school' had a certain way of getting things done without deviation. 'Old school' style called for a chain of command to be followed and expectations met without question. All involved earned the outcomes, both good and bad. Nothing was given to anyone.

In this 'old school' world, coaching players was a privilege. Players knew it was a privilege to play. When you practiced or played, pain and injury were two very different situations and were treated as such. The truth is you can practice or play through pain, but a player should **never** play through injury. In this 'old school' world, if you got your feelings hurt, you got over it. **Football is a game involving emotions not feelings. There is a big difference between the two when you are playing.**

Now, consider whether, or not, you believe 'old school' is a good or bad way to approach the game of football or life in general. Set aside your thoughts and consider another style.

The 'new school' philosophy that I've been exposed to is a more collaborative type of effort between coach and players. All parties, to some extent, have a say in the process of training, teaching and playing the game of football. In this style, as long as the job gets done, the process can be subtler and laid back. By that I mean, tough in a relaxed atmosphere. And in that process, the concern centers around the feelings of players rather than the player's emotions.

Again, consider whether, or not, you believe 'old school' is a good or bad way to approach the game of football or life in general.

If you're wondering what style I endorse, I honestly believe to be a successful coach and team of the championship caliber you need to be a combination - 'old and new school.' If you are not a physically, mentally and emotionally tough enough team, forget being championship caliber. If you and your team don't collaborate or have 'buy in' from everyone about what needs to be done to become championship caliber, the chances of your team attaining that level are slim to none, and 'slim' left the building!

Head football coaches must know their team and those players must know their coach to make certain everyone is clear on the direction of the team. *As a coach, you've got to be 'flexible, but not brittle' with players.*

It's really pretty simple. Regardless of what school you come from in your coaching style - 'old, new or combination' - you have to get it right and have buy in from all involved with the program. If you don't, you will eventually wind up coaching at 'no school.'

Takeaway #9
They Got It, You Get It, Got It!

I really don't like clutter or confusion. Actually, I prefer down right simple. But all too often we football coaches make the game that we love to teach just outright difficult. Players need you to keep it simple.

In a nutshell, I see the overriding focus of the game like this, with **'it'** being the ball. **'When they got it, you get it. When you get it, don't let them get it. You got it?'** Keep that message front and center. Ask your players to commit to it. That is football in its simplest form.

First, I understand that realistically both the player and the coach have to figure out a scheme that addresses just how to **'get it when they got it.'** Second, there must be a scheme for what to do with **it**, as well as a scheme for how to keep **it** when the opponent's goal is to get **it** back. Those two objectives require schematics, tactics and strategy. But make sure as you develop the scheme you don't out scheme yourself.

Here's where complexity can take over and upend what should be simple. In the quest to develop great schematics, remember this. **It doesn't matter what you the coach knows. But what absolutely matters is what your players know!** You may possess some of the best skills of scheme, but if your players don't understand it and absorb it you will lose every time. If you have players who are ready to learn those plays and implement them successfully that is great, but if your players are not ready to carry out your scheme and perform at a higher level then that's not so great. It will be your fault if they fail. Why, you ask? Here's why. You, the coach, made them do what they couldn't do and were not ready to do.

Take this cautionary advice. You can watch only so much game film before that film starts watching you. That is especially true in high school football. Watching film to review breakdowns and tendencies is fine. Just remember that however you choose to prepare and install your game plans, keep the player's ability to absorb that information in the forefront. Make sure there isn't any overkill. Make sure players are understanding those plans. Make sure what you are sharing is useful and leads to productivity for the team.

That may mean you need to do less scheming. A confused player will not perform nearly as well as a player demonstrating clarity when it comes to scheme. The team must be able to execute the game in its simplest form on game day. That boils down to two directives and one question.

It's really pretty simple. 'When they got it, you get it. When you get it, don't let them get it. You got it?'

Takeaway #10
A Lot of Try

Previously, I shared that my daddy was a professional cowboy in Texas. Kid Marley had many clever sayings related to his life's work with horses. One of those was, **'That horse has a lot of try in him.'** To be accurate, he sometimes would say, *'boy'* in place of *'horse.'* Anyhow, he used this phrase to express his belief that the horse gave a lot of effort every time given the opportunity. The animal just never held back, but exerted a strong inclination to do whatever was prompted in an intense way.

To me, my daddy's saying could be used to explain any player who never holds anything back when it comes to training, practice and play. The player gives his *'all-out effort'* and doesn't slack off or back off from anything. I believe that same player will not be denied the opportunity at hand. He has an inner drive that others do not have. In my opinion, most people do not have **'a lot of try in them.'** I can't tell you the reason, but I have noticed most people are set on cruise control. They seem content to let things go on by.

Well, I can't speak for anyone else, but I just don't understand, nor do I care to understand, cruise control mentality. I do, however, understand and associate myself with people who have **'a lot of try mentality.'** If you get a team full of coaches and players with **'a lot of try mentality,'** you have a great chance to attain championship caliber success.

Question: Can you pass the **'a lot of try mentality'** on to others?
Answer: It is tough, but I think you can. As a matter of fact, I know you can.

Leaders and coaches must possess the mentality first in order to pass it on to others. Next, they must demand that mentality from their team. Actions do speak louder than words, but using both actions and words to get the point across is going to be required. All coaches must set the tone for the team. Obviously, you have the ability or you would not be at that leadership level of coaching. When you get the *'a lot of try mentality'* in place, I can tell you without hesitation your team will be hard for folks to handle.

It's really pretty simple. It is really your choice as a coach. Do you want a cruise control team or *'a lot of try mentality'* team? Which will it be?

Trusting My Coach

Having someone believe in you and your talents is a gift not to be taken for granted. Rather than dismissing the advice of his high school football coach, Mickey Marley embraced it.

I always loved sports. At Franklin High School I played football, wrestled, and played baseball. To be honest I think I was a better baseball player, but I really enjoyed wrestling and football because of the physical, mental, and emotional demands it put on you. The rougher and more intense things got the more I liked it. Even as a kid I enjoyed so called 'pressure situations'. I never really looked at it as pressure anyway. Now, if someone pulls a gun or knife on you that's a 'pressure situation.' The rest is just competition, and I always embraced competition.

Well, my head football and wrestling coach was Ray Dalton. He was a prime example of how one person who takes the time to invest in a kid can change the course of that kid's life. He changed mine. Coach Dalton called the head coach at UT-Martin, George MacIntyre, and basically got him to give me a chance to walk-on his football team in the spring of 1976. One slight problem, I hadn't graduated from high school yet.

Coach Dalton and the school administration made it work so I could take enough courses in one semester to get enough credits to graduate early. I did graduate after the first semester of my senior year, and I went on to UT-Martin for the second semester that spring. It's now a common practice for incoming freshmen to enroll early but it wasn't in 1976. I made my mind up that I would go to UT-Martin, walk-on that spring and try and earn a scholarship. If it didn't work out I was going to enlist in the Marines.

Well, to make a long story short, I went, earned a scholarship, played and lettered four years, became a starter as a defensive back my junior and senior seasons and a tri-captain of the team my senior season. I graduated and coached at UT-Martin until the end of the 1985 season. Coach Dalton changed the course of my life. He knew if given the opportunity I wouldn't quit because that's what he instilled in me. Thanks Coach!

Takeaway #11
You Get What You Demand

I truly believe the statement **'you get what you demand'** is true and a vital part of who you are and what you stand for as a person and a football coach. Be certain you are clear about what this means and does not mean. Let's begin with the latter. **'You get what you demand'** does not mean being a bully or running over people to get what you want. Nor does it justify being selfish so that your needs and wants are so important all the time that you forget about the needs and wants of others. And, most of all it doesn't mean that you will crush all those around you if your demands aren't met. It means none of these.

'You get what you demand' promotes leading and coaching using a set of guidelines met daily by all those involved in your program. It requires following those guidelines consistently without deviation. Most importantly, you, the coach, and your staff are as responsible as everyone else when it comes to following those guidelines. There are no free passes for you because you are the head coach!

When you hold everyone, including yourself, to the demands of the program in place, everyone will benefit. This includes behavior. For example, what you demand of yourself is the same as what players should be expected to follow. The rules—act right, do right, be on time, do your school work—those are expectations you have for yourself and *also* your players. If they don't abide by those rules, they should be punished. Everyone involved with the program must understand that they represent their family, school, team and themselves, both on and away from the facilities. No one is exempt.

The rules set for the team are certainly to be determined by the head coach and enforcement is the coach's call every time. If the coach or any of his assistants let something 'slide by' in practice, there is a great chance your team will lose the game because the coaches allowed the 'slide' to happen in the first place. **'You get** *what you demand.'* In that particular situation, you will get a loss you deserve.

It's really pretty simple. Regardless of your rules, regulations and expectations, *'You get what you demand.'*

Takeaway #12
Do Whose Job?

Anyone who has been involved with the game of football at any level has heard a coach remind players how to carry out their assignments on the field. Three critical words and one vital directive often gets underemphasized or ignored in life and in football. **'Do your job.'** It is that simple, powerful and practical. This can be the difference between everyone's success or failure.

These three words are self-explanatory. Depending on what you decide to do, the consequences can be great or not so great. 'Do your job' means to act on what you are specifically supposed to do. That doesn't mean 'Do your job' and add someone else's job to your job. And, *by all means*, it doesn't mean 'do everyone's job on your team.' I think sometimes people, for whatever reason, forget whose job they are tasked with in the first place. Your job, executed the right way, will be enough!

The alternative will lead to massive problems, confusion, and ultimately failure to achieve championship caliber success. Consider how this simple blunder described below happened because a player chose to ignore his job.

The defensive team sets up for a specific blitz. The defensive tackle, using *3 Technique*, is supposed to go through the *B Gap*, which is between the offensive guard and tackle. The middle linebacker is supposed to go through the *A Gap*, which is between the center and guard on the same side of the defensive tackle.

All offensive gaps are covered by the defense, so, in theory, the defense has a great chance of stopping the offense. The middle linebacker deviates from his job during the play. Simply put, he decides to go through the *B Gap* and the defensive tackle does the same thing. You can imagine the outcome—not great! The offense runs the football directly at the *A Gap*, exactly where the middle linebacker should have been. As you would expect, because the middle linebacker was not doing his job, the running back has a gaping hole to run through and the result is a not-so-great touchdown for the offense. In football, the defense must make the stop!

Take care of your own business and do your job first before you try to get into everyone else's business. Too many people, in my opinion, try to put their nose where it doesn't belong in the first place.

It's really pretty simple. Do your job to the best of your ability every day. If you don't, chances are pretty good you won't have that job long anyway. So, 'Do whose job?' You decide.

Takeaway #13
Potential Will Get You Fired

You are probably thinking, what in the world does this guy mean with the statement potential will get you fired. Potential is great, right? Potential is awesome, right? **How could potential get you fired?**

First, what does potential look like? It is untapped ability, which if not tapped into by the owner, will become worthless. What value is potential if not tapped?

In the coaching world—truth be told—in every walk of life, the saying **'potential will get you fired'** holds true. A coach could have a whole bunch of players with potential, but if that coach doesn't attempt to tap that potential and use it to the very best of their God-given talents and abilities then what good is that potential? It is great to have potential. It is greater to tap it!

Many times, the one with potential doesn't really know or believe they have it. That player, student, or employee doesn't see their potential. It's possible, for some reason, they have been blinded to it over time. It is up to the coach, teacher, or leader—whomever is in charge—to try to the best of their ability to clear up any doubts.

You must be willing to push, pull, or prod, within reason, in order to get a player to tap that potential. **Most people have never been challenged enough in their lives to really live up to their full potential.** I believe some coaches do not challenge their players enough to **'tap that potential.'** If you do not challenge your players enough to 'tap that potential,' then you are doing your players a great disservice. In reality, you are not doing your job.

It is definitely a two-way street. A coach, teacher, or leader can only do so much to help someone recognize their potential and provide avenues in which that potential can be tapped.

It's really pretty simple. As a player you have a choice. Do you choose to tap your potential or do you choose to not tap your potential? After you make the choice, then what do you do? You live with it. Now, what choice do you make? It's totally up to you.

Takeaway #14
Game Plan

When a team comes together, believe me, everyone is expecting a *'game plan.'* There is no doubt about it, without a 'game plan', problems will take over down the road. If you're thinking that you've got this game plan thing covered, you just may; that is for you to decide. However, if you are not sure if having a plan is necessary, especially when it comes to the game of football, let me assure you —you're going to need a *'game plan'*. Seems pretty straightforward, but you'd be surprised how many teams try to win without one, whether that be a football team or a team of business professionals.

Every head football coach in America has a game plan for his team's upcoming opponent. Think of it like a project blueprint. The coach creates the blueprint that best fits his players' strengths and abilities. That single task is critical to the team's success. It requires preparation, a lot of detailed preparation.

For example, the head coach and his staff watch and study several game films of the opposing team. Next, they put countless hours into breaking down the tendencies that the opponent exhibits in those films. The question they must ask is, **'How could my opponent's tendencies play out in every possible game situation?'** (This includes, but is not limited to, down and distance/hash mark, position on the field, formations, motions, snap counts, and defensive fronts. It also includes coverages, in relationship to down and distance/hash mark and field position, as well as all kicking game situations.) **This is just part of what it means to prepare a game plan.**

Next, you, as the head coach, create call sheets that list each play you plan to run. These plays are based on the tendencies already identified about the opponent. Meeting with all involved, *both staff and players*, is critical to ensure that everyone knows what you have come up with. Make sure everyone understands that this is the game plan that will be executed. This meeting is the time to refine the plan if it needs it, long before you carry it out.

Here's the challenge. On game day, you may have the perfect game plan. One you believe can only run smoothly. I highly doubt it! More than likely, you will have to make adjustments to your game plan. Most assuredly, unanticipated situations will come up during the game. Be ready for that reality. If you're not, you and your team will be greatly disappointed. It is your job to adjust your game plan if necessary. Remember, you are coaching against other coaches who want to win. They have also prepared their game plans just as meticulously as you have, at least some have.

There are some head coaches, who, along with their staff, don't put in the time, effort, hard work and attention to the detail that is necessary to give their team a chance to win. No real game plan exists. This is always obvious on game day. The team seems to be aimlessly wandering around not sure of what to do. When a team gives that impression, it is usually because they don't know what to do. The team has a game plan—it's called *recipe for disaster.*

Think about it. Do you have a game plan? You may ask, *'game plan for what; I'm not a coach.'* How about a game plan for your life? You will have a much better chance of succeeding in whatever you do if you have a game plan set in place for circumstances which will inevitably arise. Will you have to adjust the game plan? Depending on the situation, and since that 'situation' is called life, the answer is absolutely yes!

It's really pretty simple. If you want to just aimlessly wander through life, not really sure of what you are doing or what you really want to accomplish, then don't prepare; you will have no game plan. If you want a chance to be successful in life then dedicate yourself to relentless preparation, attention to detail, and have a game plan.

Takeaway #15
It Ain't Work

I don't know how you classify your job, but most people I run across consider their job to be *work*. For many people, their work is what they do every day for as many hours in the day as it takes to get the job done. Each day, they do what it is they need to do to get a paycheck, and they leave their place of work when it is time to leave.

You have no idea how many people I know tell me they do just what I described every day, year in and year out. Then again, maybe you do know. One of those people I've described might be you. A job that is not really and truly what you are passionate about is not sustainable over the long haul. You will get the paycheck if you show up and do what is expected of you. You might also start to say to yourself, '**Is that it?'**

So, here is how I see it. If you find your calling in life, and make that calling your life's profession, then you really never have a job and are never really at work. You will have true passion for your calling and will not consider it a job.

You may ask, '**What is my calling and how do I find it**?' Ask yourself what it is that you really love to do in life. Of course, it must be something productive that will serve others and yourself.

Now, what is it that makes you wake up in the morning with the thought '**I can't wait to get started'.** What brings you and others enthusiasm, joy and excitement every single day? We all have something that draws out all of the feelings and excitement I just described; however, it is up to you to find that something! **That something is your calling.**

Believe it or not, it's not against the law to act upon your calling and also get paid for it. That's right! You can make a great living doing what you love to do. Personally, I found my calling thirty-seven years ago when I began coaching football and teaching. Today, I feel that over the past thirty-seven years I have never been to a **day of work**. I am not saying I didn't put in the time, effort and everything else that goes along with work in order to perfect my craft. I did what it took to try to make myself and those around me as good in our craft as we could possibly become. But it ain't work or just a job; it's my calling.

When you are really good at your calling you have the opportunity to get paid really well, and it ain't the same as work. I will be honest, if coaching football and teaching had ever become work for me then I would have given it up, because I don't believe it could have been my true calling to begin with.

It's really pretty simple. Find your life's true calling, and you'll never really work a day in your life. It ain't work; it's your calling.

Takeaway #16
'I Wish I Had Of'

I have coached football a lot of years, thirty-seven to be exact. I have also coached a lot of kids, who stayed with the games during good times and tough times. Every day wasn't the greatest experience they had ever had. But a lot of those days spent playing and practicing were foundational experiences in their lives. When it was all said and done those kids grew physically, mentally and emotionally. **They learned to push themselves beyond limits they thought possible!**

Now, football is a great game that I think every young person should have the opportunity to play if that is what they really want to do. There are some young people who never come out for the team for various reasons. There are others who start but quit the team for various reasons. I don't know any football coach who wants to see that happen, but it invariably does happen.

You have no idea how many adults I run into years after their high school days who stop me and say, *'Coach, I wish I had of stayed out for football.'* Or they may say, *'Coach, I wish I had gone out for football.'* It may sound callous, but my response is, *'Yes, but you didn't.'* And that is the truth, just as their statements to me are the truth.

These guys truly regret what they had or had not done. The reality is there is no going back. What's done is done. My point to you is, don't make your life one full of *'I wish I had of'* statements. **Make your life one of 'I am glad I did' statements.**

It's really pretty simple. We all have one life to live so live yours to the utmost. You'll be able to say, 'I'm glad I did,' instead of wish I had of!'

Takeaway #17
Does Winning and Losing Really Matter?

I believe the answer to that question really depends upon whom you're asking. If you're asking a non-competitive person that question, I imagine the answer will be *'no.'* I imagine that person might say something along the line of, *'Well, it's really more about the experiences encountered than winning and losing.'*

If you ask a competitive person that same question, I imagine the answer will be *'yes.'* That person, I think, will say something along the line of, *'If winning and losing don't really matter, why are there scoreboards?'*

I guess there are really two trains of thought about winning and losing. Everyone has the right to their own opinion, and, thankfully in the United States of America, you can give it freely. So, as a highly competitive football coach, I am going to share my opinion.

You don't last long in the football world as a head coach if you lose many games! Winning puts you on the *'fancy express train.'* Losing puts you on the *'next train out of town.'* That's just the nature of the beast. You had better win in the football world. To me, there is nothing wrong with that, as long as you play by the rules, do the right things and compete at the highest level. Do all of those and you will have a great chance of winning.

Winning is a mentality. So is losing. To be quite honest, I totally understand the winning mentality, but I do not know or care to know any other mentality. I do not know the losing mentality, nor do I care to know it. Now, having said all of that, will you win every single time you compete? No. Absolutely, not. But the person with a winning mentality will fight like he or she is going to win in everything they do. Will you lose every single time you compete with a losing mentality? The answer is yes, absolutely.

45

My original question to you was, **'Does winning and losing really matter?'**

Let's look at it this way. If you're in the business world and you 'win' a lot of accounts for your company, is that good for everybody or bad for everybody? The answer is **it's not only good, actually, it's great!**

What will happen, though, if the opposite occurs? Let's say you lose a lot of accounts for your company. Is that good for everybody involved or bad? **The answer is bad—probably terrible!** We can pick almost any 'win or lose' scenario and I promise you that to win is better every time.

I see life as a mentality, a mentality that I get to choose every single day. Guess what, so do you! I understand everyone has different situations and different environments they must deal with each day. But remember, this is the United States of America, and everyone has a right to form their own opinion and choose their mentality.

It's really pretty simple. Does winning and losing really matter? It's your choice to decide what your mentality will be.

Takeaway #18
Make the Call

If you have ever watched a football game, you probably noticed a lot of pacing up and down the sidelines by very focused coaches, all wearing their headsets. The head coach needs to be able to talk to his offensive and defensive coordinators throughout the game. It is a critically important form of communication between the different coordinators and their respective assistants. It can also be a verbal link between the head coach and all or one specific assistant.

There is a lot of communication going on, but the key is for it to be organized. Bottom line, if all try to talk at once, it sounds just like a school cafeteria full of second graders. That means chaos! It is up to the head coach to make sure all coaches know when to talk and when to listen.

Now, you are probably asking yourself, what does anything I just read have to do with *'make the call?'* Well, a lot! You see offensive and defensive coordinators make play selections and suggestions, but when it gets right down to it, especially in the crucial times of the game, it all falls on one person's shoulders—the head coach. He must *'make the call.'*

He will always ask for the best information possible from his coordinators and assistants, depending on the situation; but, ultimately, he's gotta *'make the call.'* Sometimes those headsets are burning up with selections and suggestions, sometimes not. I can say from my past experiences that they're usually not!

Most of the time, it will be you, the head coach, and you alone, who has to *'make the call.'* Truth be told that's part of being the head coach **and** being the leader. *If you don't want to 'make the call' when necessary, then you don't need to be the head coach. You don't need to be the leader.*

It's really pretty simple. You have to have courage. When the pressure is on, and everyone is depending on you, do you have what it takes to 'make the call?' You, and you alone, must answer that question. Make the call!

Takeaway #19
Box...What Box?

I know most people have heard the phrase **'think outside the box.'** You may be familiar with this challenge statement. But if you're not, **'think outside the box,'** refers to thinking of things in a different way or from a different perspective.

Well, I've heard that phrase, thought about it, and basically said to myself—'*What box?*' I never knew I was in a 'box' when I was thinking and figuring things out. *Isn't it just plain natural to think of things in new ways and try to improve upon what you've done in the past?* The answer must be *no; in fact, I know that it's no!*

As a football coach, you had better keep on top of what is new and different, whether that is the constant change of rules, strategies, schemes, or personnel. You *will* be forced to use your sense of imagination and creativity if you are going to be successful for any length of time. It's like this; you will either get yourself out of that so-called 'box' or you will most definitely fall behind, lose games and be packing a lot of boxes as you leave your former office after you get fired.

If you're worried that your self-esteem might be hurt in this process —get over it! If you don't want to face the consequences I outlined, then stay away from 'boxes.' It takes work, effort, focus, attention to detail, big-picture thinking, anticipation of the next move, and the list goes on and on. My advice is don't listen to those people who keep saying **'think outside the box,'** because, apparently, they are in the 'box.' Better yet, learn from the 'box people.' Study them to see how they got in the 'box' in the first place, and then don't do what they did to get in the 'box'

Keep your thinking fresh and do not get bogged down by the '*same old, same old*' mentality. Know your craft and your business so well that you will not be caught off guard, but instead prepared when inevitable changes must be made.

Beware that you haven't become one of those people who has created too many boxes and will soon be faced with 'moving out. 'I promise that will not be great. *Now, if you never knew you were in a box to begin with, and you don't feel the need to create a box —great. You must be staying on top of your game, improving your craft and anticipating the next change!*

It's really pretty simple. If you are in a box or, worse yet, creating boxes, stop and think about your actions. The same old, same old mentality will not keep you moving forward.

Takeaway #20
Price

When the word price comes up in a conversation, I bet the first thing you think of is money. That's only natural since in today's way of doing things most people equate *'price'* with obtaining something of material value. I can see that point of view and its validity because material things do involve a set price that must be paid.

Look at *'price'* now from a much broader perspective. There really is a price to be paid for *everything* whether or not a product or a service is exchanged. *If I've lost you, stay with me.*

For example, I'm a football coach, so I will focus on *'price'* from an athletic perspective. But, as in everything I've outlined in this book, you can substitute the role of the coach and player with your own pursuits.

'Price' is always an individual component. In the game of football, a player pays a *physical, mental and emotional price* as they train; the more they put into training, the greater the *'price.'*

There is the *'price'* of their time, depending on how many hours they devote to training. Oftentimes, people on the outside of the game overlook this pregame *'price'* paid by the player. There is the *mental and emotional price.* It increases a lot when players add in the *real* blood, sweat, and tears that occur along the way to becoming a great player. The more that player puts in, the higher the *'price'* becomes.

Not everyone is willing to pay the price. Many want to pay the price, but *few are willing* to pay the price! I ask this question a lot when I speak to groups, 'Who in here wants to be a champion?' You can imagine that almost everyone immediately throws up a hand.

My next question is, 'Who in here is willing to pay the price to be a champion?' After I explain what that price really is from a football perspective, there are not nearly as many hands flying up!

You can replace the football player with whatever activity or profession you are pursuing. I think you get the picture.

It's really pretty simple. Anything worthwhile in this world has a 'price' attached that must be paid. The choice is whether, or not, you, and you alone, are willing to pay the 'price.'

Takeaway #21
The Big Three

Without question, the three things you must personally possess to be a good or a great football player are mental, emotional, and physical toughness. I call these *'The Big Three.'* A player at these levels, both good and great, must possess *'The Big Three.'* Obviously, talent comes into play, but notice that I did not name talent to *'The Big Three.'*

I approach this from my experience in football, but you may plug in anything you do in life, and you will quickly get the picture! Here is my definition for each one of *'The Big Three.'* You must decide if and how each one applies to your situation.

First, what is 'mental toughness?' I believe this is the most important attribute one can possess in the competitive world. Basically, nothing can break your will. That means there is something inside you that touches your very soul. That something will not allow you to ever give up, no matter what is happening around you!

Bottom line: You just will not quit—ever. You will not quit regardless of the circumstances you face, including the score of the game. People with the true trait of mental toughness will not fold up like an accordion in pressure situations. People with the true trait of mental toughness are hard to find and harder to beat!

Second, what is 'emotional toughness?' Naysayers will often try to interfere with your performance, but from my perspective the one who has emotional toughness has what we call 'thick skin.' I mean skin as thick as a concrete wall. If you are in a position of leadership, criticism can be expected but so can praise. It is ultimately how you handle that criticism and praise that will determine whether you fail or succeed.

If you are a person who tries to make everyone happy, you will eventually make everyone unhappy! The key is to focus on the task at hand, regardless of what's being said about you or your team. Keep following the course you know will make you and your team successful.

Hey, all human beings have emotions, but real leaders must be able to keep theirs in check. An emotionally tough leader knows just how to harness those emotions without letting them harness him.

Third, what is 'physical toughness?' To this coach, it describes the strength to play through pain **not** injury. Let me be clear; the difference between pain and injury is critical. Pain could be anything from soreness from workouts to wearing a cast on a wrist and playing, but prior evaluation by a trainer and physician is necessary.

Injury is an evaluated circumstance by a trainer or physician with both signing off that the player should not participate in any activity until medically cleared. No player should ever be put in to a practice or in to a game situation if a trainer or physician says *no*! What the trainer and physician say is it!

To play with pain means that a player, who has been released by a trainer and physician, is given the green light to practice and play. Or, it can describe a player who has never seen a trainer or physician in the first place. All people have a different pain threshold. That is just a fact. Some can endure more than others. That is a fact. Football is a physical game played by physical people and it requires physical toughness to excel. That is also a fact.

Now, having said all of that, exactly where do you go to find mental, emotional, and physical toughness? You just can't drive to your local grocery store, go over to aisle nine and pick up some 'mental toughness.' You sure can't wander over to aisle seven for some 'emotional toughness,' and then walk over to the store clerk and ask which aisle 'physical toughness' is on.

I wish it were that easy, but we all know it isn't. For some people, it sort of defies explanation; they have just had **'The Big Three'** their whole lives. There are those people who learned **'The Big Three'** as they grew up. And for others, I have sadly found, they never have had any of **'The Big Three.'**

From my experience growing up around people who have **'The Big Three,'** I am convinced that you learn it while you're growing up and you refine it as you get older. You will want to get as many of **'The Big Three'** people on your team as you possibly can! The more people who possess mental, physical, and emotional toughness— the better your team will be.

It's really pretty simple. The more people you have on your team who possess 'The Big Three' (mental, physical and emotional toughness)—the better your team will be.

Takeaway #22
Down and Distance

'Down and Distance' is a term well known to football coaches and players. It is by this measurement that a team maintains advantage or gives up advantage. Offensive players know that in order to be successful they must obtain as many first downs as possible to maintain possession of the ball. But to be successful in that, offensive players must stay focused on *'Down and Distance'* while the defensive team does everything possible to stop them.

Now, if you aren't familiar with the game of football, you are probably asking yourself what's this *'Down and Distance'* thing? Simply put, the offense gets four tries, or **Downs**, to move the ball exactly ten yards, which is the **Distance** needed to advance. If they can't accomplish that objective, for whatever reason, the other team gets the ball. So, for example, your team is playing offense and has first down with ten yards to go. During the next play, your team gains six yards. Because you have achieved six yards on the first try, or **Down**, you are at second down with four yards to go. Every play is pivotal to achieving *'Down and Distance.'*

Having said all the above, it's pretty obvious that everyone on the field should be aware of *'Down and Distance'* at all times. Unfortunately, there is usually someone on the field who is not aware of their surroundings, meaning they ain't paying attention. Bottom line: That someone *is* clueless to what is happening around him.

In the game of football, dealing with someone who ain't paying attention or is clueless is pretty simple. The coach must quickly correct that player to where he pays attention or, as we say, catches a clue. If that doesn't get his attention, the coach must replace him with another player.

'Down and Distance' is not just a football thing. It really relates to almost everything we do in life. If you think about it, don't you

believe a person needs to know where they are in life and where they are going. To be honest, I've seen countless individuals who just ain't paying attention and are clueless in their own lives. It is a sad, but true statement.

We all have different situations in our lives, but I truly believe everyone can pay attention and catch a clue if they really want to. You ask, 'what is the key?' I think you have to really want to be engaged in what is happening around you; you are the key!

The *'Down and Distance'* in your life is up to you. Whether you get stopped on the fourth down or keep making first downs, you are the key to that. If you don't make every fourth down and sometimes turn the ball over, you must be the one to figure out a way to get the ball back and start making some more first downs.

It's really pretty simple. No matter what is happening around you, *'Down and Distance'* will be much easier to achieve if you pay attention and catch a clue. Those two concepts will serve you amazingly well your entire life!

Takeaway #23
No Fun

I think it's pretty safe to say everyone enjoys doing fun things. I would add that it's pretty safe to say no one enjoys doing things that are **'no fun!'** Now, you may be thinking 'this guy is a genius to have figured that out.' I am certainly not a genius. But through my thirty-seven years coaching football, I have figured one thing out. If you truly want to compete at a high level, and a championship level, you will have to accept there are some **'no fun'** things that must be done. There is no doubt competing at a high level is fun, and competing for a championship is fun.

If you're curious as to just what kind of **'no fun'** leads to fun things in football, I can tell you it all starts with high school football in the summer time. A player could just as easily choose to go swimming, fishing, or take it easy just hanging out with friends. In fact, there are a lot of other things players can spend time doing besides training and working out with the team every day for the chance to compete at a high level and for a championship!

Lifting weights, running and doing agility drills in the hot, humid summer doesn't seem real appealing in comparison to other things a player could do. The truth is, this is going to involve pushing and going until you think you can't go anymore. There will then be that moment when you will have to push even more!

The end result is well worth it. There will be moments when it will seem like **'no fun.'** But when you look over and see your teammates working right along beside you, that changes. All of a sudden, you realize it is well worth the sweat, effort and time you put in because the end result will make all of you perform at a higher level—*a championship level*. Now, that's fun!

I never like to sugarcoat it because you will need to approach everything you do, from workouts to practice to games, with enthusiasm and excitement. See those times as opportunities to improve. If you don't see it that way, then get out!

Only one team will win the ultimate prize—**championship**. Remember, the mentality that 'everyone gets a trophy' just doesn't exist in the real competitive world. Regardless, 'all should give their all, all the time.'

It's like my daddy used to tell me about something I would tell him I didn't like. He would look me in the eye and say **'Son, then learn to like it!'** He was a very good cowboy and I knew he didn't necessarily like everything he had to do all of the time. It didn't take me long to figure out I had to stop saying I didn't like something. That lesson from my daddy has served me well in many situations throughout the years.

It's really pretty simple. In order to get to the fun things in life, we will have to overcome some of the 'no fun' things first. I didn't say endure the 'no fun' things; I really mean *overcome* those things. There is a big difference. To me, to endure means to put up with it. To overcome means you will defeat it. It is again up to you to fully experience how 'no fun' leads to fun!

Takeaway #24
God, Family and Football

You know, to me, life is a lot about priorities. Seems the older you get, or the more experience you have, the more your priorities get shuffled around. Now, it is not my job to tell anyone how to live their life. It's just not. I do believe it is my job to share some of my life experiences with others and to give them some insight they may have never considered before.

After thirty-seven years of coaching football, my three main priorities are **God, family and football**. However, that has not always been the case. At one time early in my career it was football, football, football! I married a fantastic woman who put up with my football consumption. The key phrase is 'put up' with it.

After our daughter was born, it was football, family, football. Family did move up on the list. In my way of thinking, family was always important to me. In reality, my way of thinking was wrong. There was too much 'me' and not enough 'we.' As coaches, that is what we tell our team all the time, but I wasn't really living that at home. By the way, when I adjusted my priorities the team still won.

In my late thirties a guy by the name of Michael Sparks, who represented Fellowship of Christian Athletes, also known as FCA, started coming around to visit, and, to be quite honest, I wanted none of what he was selling.

Michael was persistent, but I finally got to where I purposefully dodged him. To his credit, he kept coming by to see me. Thank the Lord he did! He cared enough to be persistent enough to share the Word of Jesus into my life. My wife and I had always attended church; my wife, as a Christian believer, and then my daughter and me. But I was always that guy who was there in body, but on the football field in my mind.

It just so happens our pastor, Jerry Tidwell, started coming on 'house calls' about the same time Michael started coming on 'school calls.' I was thinking, *'they have me surrounded so I might as well listen to what they have to say and get it over with.'* **Again, thank the Lord, I listened**!

You know, there's a difference between hearing someone speak and listening to someone speak. Well, I listened, and my life was changed forever. I truly gave my life to the Lord and my priorities changed. My new priorities became **God, family, football.** Guess what happened next? We won football games. We won a whole bunch of football games!

I am not saying it was some kind of *'hocus pocus'* that we won a whole bunch of games because I found the Lord. I am saying, *'you can get your priorities in the right order and still be successful, happier, and live a more fulfilled life.'* At least, that's what happened for me and my family.

It's really pretty simple. Again, it's not my job to tell someone how to live their life, but I feel it is my job to share some of my life's experiences. *You are the only one who can decide your priorities in life.* **I have decided my priorities in life and they are God, family, football.**

Takeaway #25
The Grind

If you are a professional, or at the least someone who has sought out to be a champion, you probably have experienced *'The Grind.'* For you this may mean a lot of work, a lot of hours at work, and a lot of 'no fun,' time consuming stuff. There's a lot of truth in that description.

Someone, in fact, a lot of 'someones' have already gone through *'The Grind'* to become the very best possible in your field. I don't know what *'The Grind'* is in your chosen field, but I have a simple suggestion. Pick up the phone and call someone who does know!

Now, having said all of the above, let me personally share with you one bit of advice-you better beware of *'The Grind.'* If all you do day in and day out is *'The Grind,'* well, you will eventually grind yourself out of your chosen field. Some people will agree and some disagree with that last statement, but that is a matter of opinion. To me, you have to find some balance in life.

I coached football for thirty-seven years, and it was only recently that I figured this out. You might call me a slow learner. I just call myself dumb for not figuring it out earlier. In the latter years of my career, I made *'The Grind'* less of a grind, and guess what happened? We still won games. Now, it's not as if all hard work stopped and everyday was a vacation. We still got after it! We just did it in such a way that made life easier on us as coaches, and that worked in our particular situation.

To be successful in your chosen profession, you will inevitably go through *'The Grind.'* My question to you is, *Will you let 'The Grind' become such a grind that 'The Grind' eventually grinds you up?* Only you can answer that question.

It's really pretty simple. *'The Grind'* is necessary. I flat out mean *'The Grind'* is essential to success. But you don't have to lose yourself in *'The Grind.'* Stay healthy, wise, and wealthy, and find the balance in life that works for you.

Takeaway #26
Coaches Coach, Players Play, Parents Parent

Everything we do as a team must have an order to it. After all my years of coaching, this remains my firm belief. When I coached football, everything was to be done a certain way at a certain time, and nothing was to be freelanced, or basically just made up as we went along.

At the beginning of every season, we would have a team meeting, including the parents, to review team rules and expectations. **The team consisted of coaches, players, parents**. We were all part of the team!

Every team has to have a leader; that leader has to set the tone for that team. In other words, the leader has to clearly communicate what is expected and not expected of every team member. If this doesn't happen, the leader can expect chaos to occur somewhere down the road.

The head football coach is the leader of the football team. In my opinion, the leader had better make sure that everyone is aware of that fact! If he doesn't, he can expect chaos to break loose somewhere down the road, and that's a real bumpy road.

Clear communication to everyone on the team about their specific role is critical. They must know that role and know they can not deviate from their specific role. In other words, do what you are supposed to do and not what someone else is supposed to do. **Do your job**. Does that sound familiar?

When I coached, I communicated as clearly as possible at our team meetings to emphasize what everyone's specific role or job was for that season. I kept it very plain and simple.The specific roles were '**Coaches Coach, Players Play, Parents Parent'.** Now, I didn't think I could make it any clearer than that. As a matter of fact, I would specifically ask everyone during the meeting if they understood their specific roles, and if they had any questions about their specific roles. I'm not saying that as the season went on everyone always did their specific roles, but that was handled on a case-by-case basis.

To me, when any of the three specific roles gets out of whack, bad things happen.

Parents Coach equals 'not good.' *Coaches Parent* (which sometimes happens) equals 'not good.' *Players Confused by Parent Conflict with Coaches* equals 'not good.' **'Coaches Coach, Players Play, Parents Parent' equals good!**

No matter what you do in life, you have to have a clearly communicated set of guidelines to follow to keep things in an orderly fashion. I for one don't want chaos to break out when I am leading, or at any time, for that matter. Truth be told, neither do you.

You must figure out what those guidelines are, then communicate them clearly. Most importantly, you must have the guts to live by your guidelines. Be assured, somewhere down the line, you will have to back them up. There will always be people who will force you to make them understand the guidelines. In my opinion, those individuals have to be made to understand that they have two choices—get with the program or get out of the program.

It's really pretty simple. As the head football coach or leader, set your guidelines in a clear, concise manner and make sure everyone involved with the team understands and follows the guidelines of 'Coaches Coach, Players Play, Parents Parent'.

Coach Marley gravitated to football early in his career.

A Franklin High School standout, Coach Marley took his cues from Coach Ray Dalton, left. Local banker Jeff Dyer recognizes him as player of the week in the mid-70s on behalf of First American National Bank.

As a TSSAA athlete Coach Marley focused on getting the job done on the field.

A football scholarship to the University of Tennessee at Martin opened many doors for Coach Marley.

Mickey Marley's football coaching career began when he joined the staff at his alma mater UTM (second from left, kneeling).

The late Walter Kilzer, a legendary West Tennessee football coach, was a key influence on Coach Marley early in his career.

Relationships with players, parents, and community extend beyond campus for Coach Marley, here speaking to the Jackson, Tennessee Exchange Club.

While leading USJ's Bruins Coach Marley had a 245-91 record. Teammates Ryan Miller and Holland Hawks celebrate a victory. Courtesy of Mark Hawks.

Coach Marley is not shy when it comes to sharing his faith in Jesus Christ. Courtesy of Mark Hawks.

Lisa and Mickey Marley, married 28 years, share a passion for family and athletics. Courtesy of Mark Hawks.

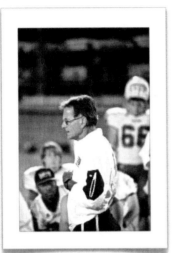

USJ players and Coach Marley pause for post-game prayer with the opposing team and coaches. Photos left and above by Mark Hawks.

Takeway #27, All We Want is All You Got, is one of Coach Marley's frequent reminders to players.

Coach Marley stands with his colleagues Mike Riggs, Robert Webber, and Franky Hodges at Trenton Rosenwald Middle School in 2018 at the Walter Kilzer Stadium.

TRMS player Kade Walker listens as Coach Marley reviews offensive plays. Courtesy of Gary Smith.

Steadfast in his principles and passion, Coach Marley strives to guide his players, always focused on 'The Big Three.' Courtesy of Gary Smith.

Coach Marley insists players must have 'The Big Three'—mental, emotional and physical toughness. Courtesy of Mark Hawks.

Players Trey Smith and Holland Hawks attempting to block a field goal. Courtesy of Mark Hawks.

'Always Look Around to See What Can Hurt You' is a principle Coach Marley instills in his players. Courtesy of Mark Hawks.

Coach Marley's career has come full circle. He now coaches in the community where his mentor gained legendary status. Courtesy of Tommy Martin.

Listening To My Coach

There is most likely at least one person in your life who has influenced who you are today. Coach Mickey Marley points to coaches like Ray Dalton and Walter Kilzer who guided him as a young player and young coach, respectively. At the heart of Coach Marley's journey, relationships make the difference.

I've been coaching football in college, high school and middle school since 1980. The one constant that runs true regardless of the level of play is relationships. I don't care what you do in life, as a profession or just as a human being, life is about relationships. Now some of my former players may read this and basically pass out seeing that I am writing about relationships. Others may not find it so strange, so let me explain myself.

Personally, I know I was not and am not the easiest person to play for, but I made no bones about it at all player-parent meetings we ever conducted. I made it quite clear that expectations would be high. Our coaches and I would accept nothing but maximum effort, attention to detail and focus on the task at hand. We would practice and play with a mental mindset and physicality that would make others not want to play us. We were a brotherhood and it was a privilege not a right to play football. We would demand more out of our players than they would think they could give. Everyone associated with the football program represented their family, school, and themselves wherever they were on the planet.

As the head coach whenever we were practicing, lifting, or doing anything of a football nature, I was all business and expected everyone else to be the same. We only had so much time to get things done and that was it.

Having said all the above I will admit I wasn't and am not an easy coach to play for, but it is never personal. That just means it is never about coaching a so-called "good kid" or "bad kid." And my intent was never to blatantly get on to someone for no reason. I am sure there were times when a player may have felt like that, but it's never personal. Football is a hard sport and difficult to play. You must do your job individually well. More importantly, you must do the job collectively well as a unit, as a team.

Some of my best moments in football happen off the field especially as I get older. I have young men call, text, or write to me about how playing football in high school helped them grow from a boy to a man. I have some say they couldn't stand me then but now, ten, fifteen, twenty years later, they understand. Most importantly, what they tell me is what they learned from playing football has helped make them a better husband, father, and man. I enjoy being invited to their weddings and seeing them, their bride, families and former teammates. I really enjoy that!

In a nutshell, I have had a great career and made friends with many coaches across the United States. Above all, I know for a fact I have made relationships and bonds with young men that will last a lifetime. That is what makes coaching football so great. Simply put, it is the relationships of people. Ultimately, it is about knowing that you can count on them *and* them knowing they can always count on you!

Takeaway #27
The Right Thing

What does *'the right thing'* really mean? I guess if you asked a hundred people that question, you may get a hundred different answers. I've heard the old saying, 'You'll never go wrong doing the right thing.' To be honest with you, I truly believe that saying. Problem is—how do you know what *'the right thing'* is?

I am certainly no psychologist. I am a football coach, so I am making a lot of summations here that I truly believe. You will have to make your own.

There are obviously set laws, rules, and regulations that we are to live by and put in place for the well-being of our society. Prisons are full of murderers, thieves, and drug dealers. Those are obvious criminal acts that are not to be tolerated. You would think common sense would prevail with basic rules like *'Don't lie, cheat or steal.'* So, it seems to me more common sense than anything else that we would all hear the call to *'be kind, courteous and respectful of people.'* I mean what is 'not right' about that? We can all be kind, courteous and respectful to people.

Now, back to the original question on *'the right thing.'* I believe deep down inside ourselves, we know what *'the right thing'* really is. We know if something deep down inside just feels wrong then it is wrong. So, I would bet that most people *do know* what *'the right thing'* really is. It's just a matter of whether we will do it or not.

As a football coach, I can guarantee you the more people you have on your team that will do *'the right thing,'* the better your team will be. Notice, I didn't mention anything about 'talent,' which obviously helps. I am referring to people who will do *'the right thing.'*

It's really pretty simple. If you truly want to be successful in whatever you do, then do *'the right thing.'*

Takeaway #28
All We Want Is All You Got

There is a short, simple phrase that is easy to say but difficult to accomplish. It's a phrase that, if totally accomplished in the football world by a player and team, will bring about huge benefits for all. As a matter of fact, it's a phrase that, if a person in any circumstance will actually do, will bring about huge benefits.

So, what's the phrase you ask? *'All we want is all you got.'*

It is really as simple as that. It's not hard to understand, not hard to figure out. Again, you ask, *'what does it mean?'* It means, *'All we want is all you got.'*

In the football world, we as coaches want every player on the team to give 100 percent of himself in everything he does. That means in academics, workouts, practice, games, and off the field activities. Now, last time I looked, 99 percent, 98 percent, 97 percent isn't 100 percent.

So, you may be asking, *100 percent of what?* I already told you— *100 percent of himself, or yourself—100 percent effort.* *'All we want is all you got.'*

How many people actually give 100 percent effort in what they do? You would think most do, right? The answer is **most do not give 100 percent.** Most people may think they are giving 100 percent, but they actually are not.

Now, in the game of football, you have the advantage of going back after the game has been played and reviewing every play on film. I will guarantee you that some players will not be giving 100 percent on every play, especially in high school. They may have thought they were during the game, but the film shows otherwise. As they say in the football world, *'that eye in the sky don't lie.'*

I will also guarantee you that, regardless of what you do or see others do, most people aren't giving 100 percent effort every time. Of course, most people don't have the ability to look back on a film of a previous performance, so how will you know if you are giving 100 percent? You will know when other people start getting dissatisfied with your job performance or the boss calls you in for a 'get right or get gone talk.' Trust me. You will find out pretty quickly from others whether or not you are giving 100 percent or not.

So how do you *'condition or train'* yourself to give 100 percent all the time? Well, it's easy. **Give all you got all the time. You have to make yourself do it. Never settle for anything but your best in everything you do.**

That may sound very difficult to do, and guess what? **It is difficult.**

It's why most people don't give 100 percent effort every time. Most people like the easy way of doing things, and, just basically, look for ways to cut corners. Most people avoid things that require actual effort and work. These same people will eventually find one thing they can't successfully avoid – *loss of playing time as a player*. And as they step out of the football world and into the career world, these same people, who refuse to give 100 percent, won't be able to avoid the loss of a job.

It's really pretty simple. You either will or you won't give 100 percent all the time. You should decide what type of person you want to be: 'a 100 percent player,' or 'someone just like the rest of them.' I am going to tell you that the decision on what we, as coaches and leaders, want from you has already been made. 'All we want is all you got.'

Takeaway #29
Practice

What does *'practice'* actually mean? Football coaches believe it means to repetitively prepare the team for the next game or season. Players also know it means preparing—repetitively preparing—the team for the next game or season. Just how those practices are actually implemented by coaches and carried out by players will vary from team to team.

You and I know that doctors *'practice'* medicine. I have had several operations over the years, and, to be quite honest with you, at no time did I want anyone *practicing* on me. I told the nursing staff that just as they were giving me anesthesia, or basically knocking me out, before my surgery. The last thing I remember hearing that day was laughter, so I was hoping that was a good sign!

As a coach, however, practicing means you may try different things. Because some things will work and others will not work, you get rid of what doesn't work. When I was a patient, I didn't want 'amateur hour' practice. Fortunately, I had great physicians and nurses, putting me, the patient, in good hands.

All of the above may sound like rambling, but stay with me. The point I am trying to make is practice is done by basically everyone. Students repetitively study for their particular subject. Doctors, lawyers, teachers, coaches, and other professionals study their field to keep up with the most updated materials and procedures. However, in football, 'the tale of the tape,' as they say, is how one practices. In other words, *is it well thought out, performed in a timely manner, detail-oriented and focused?* Or, is it just the opposite?

Does it really make any difference how you *practice*? Well, you had better believe, and I mean 100 percent believe, that it does. **You and your team will play and perform the same way you and your team practice.** If you and your team practice in a timely, orderly fashion with a sense of purpose, attention to detail and focused intensity, you and your team will have a chance to be successful in a good competitive environment. *Yes, how you practice matters.*

It's really pretty simple, regardless of your field of study or chosen profession, the way you practice will determine your success. *The test a student takes, the presentation given at work, and the football game itself are all the end results of practice.* Of course, as a coach, it's totally up to you how you choose to practice, but make sure everyone involved with your program understands that practice is important.

Takeaway #30
No Excuses

Guess what is the easiest thing in the world to make? Well, it's an excuse.

Anybody can make one, and most people do. It's easy to come up with a reason why you didn't do something or to blame someone else for something you did or didn't do. **Yes, the world is full of 'excuse makers!'** Now, you may be thinking that everything that has been said so far seems pretty harsh. All I can say is, **'If you are an excuse maker, then I guess it is.'**

You see, truth be told, nobody wants to hear about how you couldn't do something or why someone or something stopped you from doing whatever it is you were supposed to do. Here's a reality check. **'Nobody wants to hear excuses except other excuse makers.'**

You may have noticed that at no time have I mentioned the fact that it cannot be debated. **You will run into obstacles doing whatever it is that you do**. Trust me on this one. Things are going to happen, good and bad. You just should deal with it. It goes back to a phrase I emphasized in an earlier takeaway: 'Do your job.'

I guarantee you nobody will want to hear you complain, gripe, or make excuses. Like it or not, all of us are being evaluated by something or someone. Whether we are at home, at work, or out in the community, we are being evaluated. So, what does that mean? Well, as a football coach you are evaluated by wins and losses. Like it or not, that's the way it is.

Believe me, nobody wants to hear any excuses why the team lost the game. They just don't. As a business person, nobody wants to hear any excuses why you lost an account. They just don't. A school teacher doesn't want to hear any excuses why a student didn't do the homework assignment. They just don't. We can go on and on, but I think you get the point.

Now, at no time did I say mistakes would not be made, because we are all human. Believe it or not, mistakes happen. The thing is nobody wants to hear any excuses about the mistakes. **Own the mistakes and don't make excuses**.

Again, you may think that's a little harsh, but let me ask you a question. Is it harsher than hearing the words 'your services are no longer required with our company?' You decide what you think is the best option—excuses or no excuses.

It's really pretty simple. Nobody wants to hear excuses. If you are an excuse maker, stop.

Takeaway #31
Hustle

What is hustle? Well, hustle is just plain outright relentless effort. That's it in a nutshell. **Hustle doesn't require talent, but it does require drive, motivation, courage, and plenty of guts.** As a football coach, if I have to choose between a player who has talent, but no hustle, or a player with less talent, but plenty of hustle, I will take the second player all day long.

When a coach has a player with talent and hustle, well, he's got a special player. Now, you are probably asking yourself why I would take hustle over talent. I am going to tell you why. Talent will only take a person so far. Talent is great, but eventually that person with talent will be thrown in with other players with talent and they will all look the same. There will be no difference between any of them.

Let's take an example of a player in middle school football who is just better than everyone else. He relies on talent alone and nothing else. Then he goes to high school and the same thing happens. He's just better than the rest. Let's say that player goes on to college where everyone has talent and that player must actually compete for a spot on the team. Now, for the first time in his life, he must rely on something more than talent alone to make it, but until that moment he has never had to find that hustle.

It's basically like throwing cold water in someone's face. It's a shock to that player that his talent alone won't be enough for him to make it. Some wind up adjusting and becoming good to great players. Some wind up leaving because they just don't know how to handle the totally *new situation* they are facing—the situation that there are *others who also have talent.*

Now, using the same scenario, let's take a player who has less talent, but also has hustle. This second player will find a way to make it because he has always had to find a way to make it. Now, he may not be a star or even a starter on his middle school and high school teams, but he finds a way to contribute to the teams. **Now, he may have to walk on to try out for a college football team, but, in some cases, the player with hustle makes the team.** Now, this isn't fantasy camp, so the odds are stacked against a walk on to make the team. But some do. They can become a vital part of that team, and it was pure hustle that got them there.

Point being, the more people you have on the team with hustle the better the team will be. When you combine talent and hustle, and you have a lot of those players on the team, then everyone on the schedule had better watch out. I think you get the picture. I don't care what you are doing; people with hustle will make your team or organization better.

It's really pretty simple. Talent with no hustle is not great. Talent combined with hustle is great. If you want to make your team or organization better then have a lot of people that will hustle.

Takeaway #32
Basics

Basics are the bare necessities needed to function in anything one does. Try not breathing for a while and see where that gets you. Breathing is a necessity to live. That's pretty much one of the basics of life. Now, let's use some football analogies. The very basics of the game of football are blocking, tackling, running, passing, catching, and kicking. These basics must be properly practiced and mastered by those involved in the game.

Different position players will practice certain basics of the game more than others, but, as a general rule, the very basics of the game must be mastered. Now, the question is *how long does it take to master the basics?* **I believe the answer is a lifetime. As long as you are involved in football, the basics must always be practiced.**

It amazes me that some coaches will get caught up in plays and schemes so much so that they move away from the basics of the game. To me, if you have a lousy blocking and tackling team, it really won't matter what plays or schemes you run because the team is going to lose anyway!

Let's talk academics. I believe two of the basics are being able to read and write well. Now, if you can't do either of those two things well, then I would pretty much bet the chances of you excelling academically are not great. If you have mastered those basics the chances of you excelling academically are great.

I really don't care what you set out to do. **I believe you must discipline yourself to master the basics.** Now, how long did I say I thought it took to master the basics? **It takes a lifetime.** Will it be repetitive? The answer is yes. Will it sometimes get monotonous? The answer is yes. Will there be times when you think, *'I already know all of this, so what's the use?'* You may, but I hope not.
Because when you think you know it all, problems occur because you don't know it all.

It's really pretty simple. The 'greats in the competitive world,' regardless of what they do, are always striving to master the basics. In other words, you should always have plenty to do, especially since *it takes a lifetime to master the basics.*

Takeaway #33
Don't Take Financial Advice from Broke People

Throughout my thirty-seven years of coaching football, it always amazed me how much advice I got, whether I wanted it or not. Then again, I know that's just what comes with the territory. *Isn't it amazing how other people think they know more about your job than you.* To be quite honest, ninety-nine percent of the advice I got 'went in one ear and right out the other,' as the saying goes. Now, was that because I was hard-headed and thought I knew everything? Some would say, 'yes.' But the answer is *no*, definitely not.

Basically, it's just like this. Those advice givers were clueless about what they were talking about. **However, I made it a point to always listen to those who I believed did actually know what they were talking about.** In fact, I often sought out others in my field, if for no other reason but to bounce things off them or to exchange ideas pertinent to our situations. Now, when needed, that practice included giving and taking advice.

Sharing ideas among colleagues in your chosen profession can be very powerful! Seeking the counsel of wise people is smart. Listening and applying the advice of wise people is smart. Listening to and applying the advice of people who only think they know what's best is dumb. **You see, many think they know, but only a few really do.**

Remember, there is a difference between hearing someone and listening to someone. You can't help but hear unless you have a hearing problem. But when you hear advice over and over again that is both unsolicited and not good, eventually the words become clanging symbols to your ears, making noise that clutters your mind. And, trust me on this, you will train yourself to tune out that noise.

You can and should listen to what you really want to know. **You will tune in, not out, to soak up as much good information as**

possible. Over the years, I have trained myself when to listen and when not to listen. The thing is, it's very liberating!

I had a fella give me some great advice a long time ago, and I chose to listen. The great advice was *'don't take financial advice from broke people'* Now, that advice was direct, simple, and made perfect common sense to me. You know what? I am sure glad I chose not to just hear his advice, but also to listen to his advice.

It's really pretty simple. You will receive advice from a lot of folks who think they know your business better than you. I guarantee you will hear it all, but it's up to you to whom you will listen. My advice is don't take financial advice from broke people. My friends, this advice I'm sharing covers a whole lot more ground than just finances. But I'll bet by now you have figured that out!

Takeaway #34
Time

I think the most valuable asset a person has is time. There are seven days in a week, twenty-four hours in a day. That's a total of 168 hours, 10,080 minutes, or 604,800 seconds in a week. That sounds like an awful lot of time, but is it, really? I hear people say, '*I never have enough time.*' You know, those people may just have more of a time management problem than an actual time problem.

As a veteran football coach, I can assure you that time management was one of my keys to success. If we had a two-hour football practice, then every second of every minute of those two hours was scripted. Everyone—coaches, players, equipment staff— knew exactly what we would be doing during that 120-minute period of time. We didn't just roll a ball out on the field and say, '*Do what you want for two hours.*' That is called recess not football practice!

Hours upon hours were put into preparation for any given team practice. You play a different opponent each week, so coaches watch hours of game film to prepare. The staff meets to make sure no stone is left unturned when getting ready for that opponent. The coaches make out game plans, individual group plans, and travel itineraries, among other tasks.

Time management is the key. It is not about the amount of time you spend doing something; it is about how you utilize your time.

I know some staffs that spend all their time at the office, but really don't get much accomplished. I know other staffs that spend less time at the office and get a whole lot accomplished. One is a time waster, the other is a time user.

Bottomline: Don't be a time waster. That goes for everybody regardless of who you are or what you do.

It's really pretty simple. We all have one life to live on earth; we only have so much time. Give yourself a great gift and maximize the time that you do have. Make time management a priority in your life!

Takeaway #35
Pressure

Did you know diamonds are formed from a great amount of earth's pressure? My wife loves diamonds. Personally, I love pressure situations.

Imagine, you're coaching a game. Your team has the ball on a last possession, and in a two-minute drive they win the game that will take them to a state championship. Man, that's awesome!

Now, there is all kinds of pressure, some good and some not so good. I guess it just depends on how you look at it. Air pressure in your tires is good or your vehicle wouldn't go anywhere. Air pressure in a hot air balloon is good or you wouldn't want to be up in one when the pressure gives out. A blood pressure of 110 over 70 is a good, healthy number for your body.

I think it is pretty clear that not all pressure is bad, so why is it that most people get an uneasy feeling when they hear the word pressure? Is it that most people equate pressure with any of some zillion things, mostly bad, that they think could happen? I would guess probably so, but then again, I am not a *'guessamatologist.'* *I do know that some people handle pressure better than others, and some handle it a lot better than others.*

I guess there is a fear of failure, which makes some of us handle pressure worse than others. While coaching football, I have seen players and coaches crumble under pressure and others be cool as cucumbers. I prefer cucumbers.

Pressure situations are a time to rise up and get the job done! It's a time to test yourself and those around you. Pressure is a mindset to the true competitor. The tougher the challenge, the tougher the mindset gets. Pressure situations are not feared by the true competitor, but embraced. *There is no fear of failure because there's no fear at all, just pure focus on the task at hand.*

One thing is for sure—at some time in our life, pressure will come our way. So, the question is, *'will you crumble or be the cucumber when you have to face the pressure?'*

It's really pretty simple. Pressure is something that most people really don't want in their lives, meaning it is avoided at all cost. Now, to others pressure is something that is embraced. I can't speak for you, but pressure situations are just outright fun to me!

Takeaway #36
Gettin' It

Ever heard the phrase, *'If I ain't gettin' it, they ain't nobody gettin' it?'*

Well, probably not, but I sure have. You are probably asking yourself, 'What in the world does that phrase mean?' Let's break it down so everyone can understand it.

'I' means *you*. Simple enough. *'Ain't'* means *not*. Simple enough.

'Gettin' it' means *working*. Simple enough. *'They ain't nobody gettin' it'* means *nobody's working.*

So, the entire phrase is saying, *'If you are not working, then nobody is working.'* It simply means that *'nobody will out work you.'*

Now, to me, that's a great phrase!

This is short and to the point. People, teams, organizations, and all the rest that are consistently successful are always *'gettin' it.'* Everybody else is just standing or probably just sitting around watching.

It's really pretty simple. There's no beating around the bush on this one! Let the standers stand and the sitters sit around and watch the ones working become successful because they are always *'gettin' it.'*

Takeaway #37
You've Gotta Produce

I read an article in the newspaper the other day about an assistant football coach in the NFL. He talked a little bit about his job and what it entailed. He also made the point that he is in a *production business*. That simply means his team had better win a lot of games or the coaches will be looking for other coaching jobs. Now, after saying all that I want you to think about something. **Who is not in a production business?**

Try being bad at what you do for a while and see what that gets you. *I can tell you: It gets you fired!* Like it or not**, you've gotta produce**. Now, the crazy thing about it is you can actually do a good job and still get fired.

'What?' you say. 'Well, yes,' I say. It happened to me.

Without getting into many details, my life changed abruptly after twenty-seven years as a head high school football coach. Coming off a 9-4 state semi-final season, I was brought in two days after our football banquet and asked to step down as the head football coach. I was told the decision had nothing to do with our team record, wins or losses, but that the administration wanted to go in a different direction. Hey, no problem! *I knew I had done my best and given all I could give. What was done was done, and that was it.,*

You're probably saying to yourself, 'What does **you've gotta produce** *really mean if you can be fired either way?'* Well, what happened to me was a rare case, which usually doesn't happen. *I can, however, guarantee you of a not so rare case. If you don't produce, you will be fired.*

I don't care what you do, you've gotta produce or you will be gone. That may cause some hurt feelings; sorry, but it's the truth. I, personally, don't let others define me or define my self-worth. I hope you don't either. *I just do my best every day in whatever I am doing and keep moving.*

I am constantly trying to learn something new every day that will make me better at my profession. I hope you are also. *I personally don't fear failure. I didn't say I like failure. I said I don't fear failure.* When we do fail, and we all will, we have two choices: whine about it or correct the mistake and move on. My choice is the latter. What is your choice?

It's really pretty simple. Regardless of who you are, or what you do, the plain fact of the matter is you've gotta produce. *So, don't find just a job; find your passion and do that as your profession. When you do, you will enjoy, excel, and produce. Believe it or not, you can do it!*

Takeaway #38
Football, The Great Equalizer

I have always loved the game of football. Ever since I was a little kid, I have just loved the game. What I really love is the physical aspect of football. Truth be told, I just loved hitting people! **You know, when you're a kid you just play. To me, that's great. You learn the rules of the game as you grow; but, no matter what, you just play.**

I was fortunate enough to play football from middle school through college. Through the years my love for the game never changed. As I said, I loved to just play and hit people; yet, I also learned something very important. **Football is the great equalizer.**

What does that exactly mean? Well, to me, it means that everyone who is playing has a clean slate, no matter your race, your religion, or your socioeconomic background. **Everyone has a fair chance to show what they can do.**

I can't speak for you, but I can speak for me; that's the way it was on every football team I ever played for growing up and in college. Eventually, I became a football coach. That's the way it has been on every team I have ever coached in my more than thirty-seven year career.

Now, I was never in one offensive or defensive huddle where someone said, *'Let's give the ball to the black guy or white guy or Asian guy or Latino guy.'* What we did together was what made us a team. We came together, we listened for the play to be called, and we ran the play. It was that simple. None of us cared about skin color, religious background or how much money an individual player had or didn't have.

All we cared about was getting the job done, playing the game. We were all equal as players.

That was not to say our individual talents were equal because they weren't. I played with a lot of amazing athletes much more talented than me, but as teammates we were equal. **We respected one another for what we could bring to the team, as well as for our strengths as individual players.**

The only color we saw was the color of the school uniforms we represented. **We were a brotherhood brought together by our love of the game of football and what each one of us as individuals could offer the team.** That very same brotherhood, brought by our love of the game of football, brought us together and caused us to love our teammates through the game of football. Collectively, we didn't care about anything else except our teammates and the team. Now, if that's not what equal means, then I really don't know what it does mean.

If you want to see great equality, unity, and brotherhood, then watch a great football team. Better yet, bring those attributes to your team, regardless of your occupation.

It's really pretty simple. **I know for a fact that anyone who has ever really played the game of football would agree with me in saying that** *football is the great equalizer.* **Now, imagine if you took the word football out and replaced it with your occupation or organization. How great would that be?** *The possibilities are endless.*

Lessons Learned

No one is ever truly prepared for a jolt that seems a bit like a rear end collision. Coach Mickey Marley, who made it a priority to always be prepared and ready for the next opponent on the field, did not anticipate the professional change coming his way in 2015.

There is an old saying in the football coaching business *'If you haven't been fired just wait, you will be'*. It's gotta be true because it happened to me twice.

First time was fall of 1985 when our staff was let go at UT-Martin after the season. I played there from 1976 until 1979, coaching there until 1985. I really enjoyed my time at UT-Martin. I got a good education, made life long friends, had a good playing career and learned a lot about coaching football from some really good coaches.

Well, time moves on. It was time for me to move on except for one thing, I had no where to go. I basically bounced around from friend to friends' houses for about six months. I sold my watch, gold ring and chain at a pawn shop in Nashville for $150. Guess what I did with the money? You're right. I went to a junk yard and bought a car for, you guessed it, $145. I had five dollars left for gas.

What kind of car could you get for $145? Well, I'll tell you, not a Corvette. It was a gold 'Scamp'! It had a hole in the bottom of the floorboard, so I could see the white stripes of the highway as I was driving. It was like the 'Fred Flintstone' mobile.

Anyway, to make a long story short I drove to a hotel in Nashville where the state high school coaching convention was being held. I met Coach Walter Kilzer from Jackson, Tennessee. He was coaching at what was at the time Old Hickory Academy. Coach Kilzer hired me as his defensive coordinator and off to Jackson I went.

Now, I didn't know anything about Old Hickory Academy, but I knew I had a job so that was a big plus. To show you how things work out, Old Hickory Academy and Episcopal Day School merged one year after I got there becoming University School of Jackson. Coach

Kilzer, who I consider a great mentor, retired. In 1989 I became the head football coach. That year we won the first playoff game in school history and for the next twenty-seven years we were 245-91, played in five state championship games, ten semi-final games and a lot of quarter-final games. Along the way I made many great friends and worked with a lot of outstanding coaches, teachers and administrators.

The greatest thing that happened was I met the 'Love of my Life', Lisa. We have been married 28-years. We have a beautiful daughter Jordan. Guess who was best man in our wedding? That's right—Coach Walter Kilzer.

In 2015 our team was 9-4 and went to the state semi-finals. A few weeks before Christmas I was told the school was 'going in a different direction,' and I was let go as the head football coach. I did nothing morally or ethically wrong. This being the United States of America, the greatest country ever, where all have the right to make their own decisions, I knew the decision had been made. I had a great career at University School of Jackson and enjoyed my time there. I really appreciated the players and coaches with whom I had coached and worked with throughout the years. No regrets! I stayed one more year and taught then took another coaching job in 2017.

Talk about the ironies of all ironies. We continue to live in Jackson, but I became the head football coach at Trenton Rosenwald Middle School in Trenton, Tennessee. It's about thirty minutes from home, no big deal. I had never coached players this age before so it was and is a fun, different experience for us all. Good kids who try hard to do their best. Great school, teachers, administrators and community.

Here's the ironic part. The game field is named after guess who? You got it—Coach Walter Kilzer! That's right. The very man who brought me to Jackson in 1986 and was best man in our wedding. See Coach Kilzer is a legend especially in Trenton. He went to Trenton schools, was a great athlete, played at Vanderbilt and at Georgia Tech during World War II for legendary Coach Bobby Dodd. Coach Kilzer eventually came back to Trenton and coached the high school football team for thirty years. He coached middle school and high school football at Old Hickory Academy and then University School Jackson.

So, here I am coaching middle school football at the latter part of my career at the stadium named after the coach who brought me to Jackson, mentored me working with high school age players, and was best man in our wedding!

Now I can't speak for you, but I can for me. Whenever you face change don't run from it. Face it and move on. You never know that very change may lead you to the *'Love of your Life'* and a great career to boot!

Takeaway #39
Less is Better Than More—Really

You have probably heard people say, *'Less is better than more.'* That can seem a little backward when you're young, and even as you get older. I know less money isn't as good as more money. I know less time isn't as good as more time. I know less fun isn't as good as more fun.

We could play this game all day, so what does *less is better than more* really mean? Well, I guess less is better than more really depends upon what you're doing? I'm going to take this from a football coach's perspective and you take it from yours. I'll bet we both get it.

As a football coach, you need your team to be as prepared as possible, and with today's technology that includes computer analysis of opposing teams' offenses, defenses, kicking game and anything else you want. Plus, you need to implement your system of plays, but also be ready to start changing things around to try and get the perfect plays to win the game.

That's all great if your team can actually absorb and execute all the information you give them. It's not great if they can't. There is this phrase, *paralysis by analysis.* It shows up when you are so overloaded with facts, figures, and data that you can't do anything. This is something that a lot of football coaches are guilty of doing to their teams, especially in high school.

The coaches overload their team with so much information that the players can't read and react in the game. In other words, the players start thinking instead of doing. The flat fact of the matter is: it doesn't matter how much information you and your coaches know; it matters how much information your players know and can execute.

In other words, there comes a time when less is more. Hey, you *need* to cut down on the data and focus on execution. It really doesn't matter if you have a lot of plays if you can't execute them. Don't go to your next coaching clinic and be the dumbest, smart guy in the room. (In other words, you were dumb by trying to make your team so smart that they couldn't execute.)

It's really pretty simple. Information and knowledge are powerful tools. Learn to use those tools to your advantage. Don't try to be so smart that you wind up being dumb. *You, and the team, will be a lot better off when you learn that sometimes less is better than more, really!*

Takeaway #40
Is This Competitive?

How many times have you, as a coach, been asked, **'Is this competitive?'** I have heard a lot of parents say, **'Is this sport, or that sport, a competitive sport or non-competitive sport?'** I'm gonna tell you that is a question that has been posed to me over the years that just doesn't make sense. I understand what is being asked. But what I don't understand, nor do I want to understand, is the mindset that comes up with this question.

If people are involved, and there is some sort of game involved, like it or not, there is competition involved. Now, you have to choose whether to accept it, but that's just the way it is.

Earlier, I made a point of talking about competition and how parents of younger children sometimes go crazy with competition before kids are ready. The fact of the matter is, however, someone is always keeping score, so you better learn to deal with it. My advice to everyone is: learn to love it.

Think about this. Is it competitive for a student to get into a college? Yes. Last time I looked, test scores such as the ACT and SAT, as well as a student's GPA, absolutely matter in college admission. In reality, your child has been competing all their academic life. If that surprises you, consider this: **people are involved and scores are kept, hence, competition exists.**

Whether or not you choose to embrace competition is completely up to you. Embrace it or not; the competition is there.

It's really pretty simple when you get right down to it. Most of

the greatest things in life are competitive, meaning *you will be challenged to do your very best and give your all. You had better be ready. I will guarantee you that the game of life is competitive, so my advice is simple - enjoy and compete!* It's one game in which everybody will participate, so embrace and enjoy it because this game, the game of life, is competitive.

Takeaway #41
Heart

Well, I would say that one of, if not, the most vital organ in the human body is the heart. When working properly it keeps the blood flowing to the other organs in your body. ***Basically, it helps run the most amazing creation of all time, and that creation would be you and me.***

Now, I am not a cardiologist, but I know that the heart can be examined through a battery of tests for its functionality. You can have blood work, stress tests, an EKG, echo-cardiograms, heart caths and more to check out your heart. If it sounds like I know something about the testing part, I do, because I had all of the fore mentioned performed on me.

It's amazing what modern medicine can do today. I had two stents put in to fix ninety-eight percent and seventy percent blockages of my heart. I was out of the hospital in two days and doing great. ***Yes, the heart is truly amazing.***

There's a different kind of heart that's also truly amazing. ***The heart of the competitor. The heart of the winner. The heart of the champion***. Now, we are talking about a different type of heart. As a football coach, you can quickly assess when a player does or doesn't have this kind of heart.

More important than speed, agility, quickness, and size is the heart of a player. You may ask '*What is it about this heart that is so much more important than anything else a player may possess?*' Well, I am gonna tell you.

This heart is drive, courage, commitment, persistence, loyalty, toughness, refusal to accept anything but best effort, and flat out guts in all phases of life. ***Heart is a mindset.*** Heart will eventually defeat talent alone every time. If you get a team with a combination of heart and talent then you have something special.

To me, the one thing that gets overlooked more than anything else in player evaluation is heart. Obviously, a certain degree of talent is required to achieve success, regardless of your given profession. *Never forget that heart, or the of lack of heart, really does matter.*

It's really pretty simple. Physically, our heart pumps life-giving blood into our body. Well, players with heart will pump life-giving blood into the team or organization. Hey, talent matters, but don't forget, so does heart.

Takeaway #42
What Does Control Really Mean?

Is it that you have *total command* of a situation? Is it that you have *some command* of the situation? Or, is it that you don't want anything to do with the situation in the first place? In other words, you *avoid command.*

Here is the best way I can describe for you what control really means to me. Have you ever been on the back of a horse that was runnin' away? Well, first of all, for those of you who don't have a clue as to what that feels like, it is when a horse takes off running at full speed and will not stop. Sounds like fun, right. Well, wrong!

That horse will run you into fences, trees, ditches, and just about anything else blocking its path. I have been on the back of a *runaway horse,* and believe me when I tell you there is nothing quite like it. In a split second, you know that *if you don't take control of the situation that horse will.*

You have some options, but your options are limited. *What's worse, time is not on your side.*

First option: You can jump off. Let me advise you, don't do that.

Second option: You can stay on and let that horse run you into fences, trees, ditches, and anything on its path. Don't do that.

Third option: You can rope or lasso a tree stump like one of our friends did years ago. Let me tell you, *for sure,* don't do that.

Here's your final option: *Take control of the situation. Do that!*

This is what I know from my own experience with a runaway horse. What you do is reach down as far as you can on the left-hand side of the reins and start getting that horse to going in circles. Eventually, that horse will slow down, and you won't get yourself involved in a painful wreck.

The runaway story is an example of *you taking control*. Personally speaking, I can tell you my personality lends itself to being in control. Now, not everyone is built that way. I emphasized earlier *'you gotta be you,'* so all I'm saying is *somebody's gonna be in control or you'll have complete chaos.*

You, as an individual, have to decide what you want. Teams and organizations have to decide what they want when it comes to who is in control. All I know, if there is no captain runnin' the ship that ship will crash and sink. I'll give you one better. If you let that horse you are riding run away, guess what? It will. And, what's worse, it will get you hurt.

It's really pretty simple. Someone, or something, is going to be in control. You have a lot more decision-making power in that control than you think. It's just a matter of how you handle control and the situation facing you.

Takeaway #43
Want vs. Willing

I made this statement earlier, but I think it bears repeating. I often would ask my players this question: *'How many of you want to be a champion?'* Everybody immediately would throw their hands up.

Next question. *'How many of you are willing to do what it takes to become one?'* Again, everybody would throw their hands up.

Now, when talking to a high school football team most players understood the questions asked and threw their hands up due to their true conviction. Some didn't really understand the questions asked and threw up their hands mainly because everyone else did.

We, as coaches, always made sure that all involved with the team eventually understood those questions. How did we do that? The answer is simple. We, as coaches, demanded everyone's best effort at all times.

The difference between 'want vs. willing' is huge, and as coaches, we know that to be true. It is our job to make sure all involved with the team learn the difference.

So, for instance, you say you want a Mercedes. That's great. Well, are you willing to do what it takes to get one? You know, like all things, it comes with a price tag.

Or, maybe **you want to be a doctor or lawyer.** Again, that is great. But are you willing to do what it takes to be a doctor or a lawyer?

Now, you just raised your hand to say that you want to be a championship caliber football player. The question is, *'Are you willing to be a great teammate?'* And, as coaches, we must ask the team this question. *Are all of you truly committed; committed to giving all you got in every lifting session, workout, team meeting, practice session, your actions on and away from the field, academics, and games?* This list certainly can go on and on.

If one is willing to truly 'pay the price' in whatever they are doing then they have a great chance for success. If one is not willing to 'pay the price' in whatever they are doing then they have a lousy chance for success. I mean lousy.

The true champions in any field of endeavor are sure of what they want and are willing to go get it. The question you must answer is *'Do you know what you want and are you willing to go get it?'* There is a huge difference between 'want vs. willing.' You decide the difference for you.

It's really pretty simple. Successful people, in whatever field they choose, don't luck into it; they work into it. That work is a lifetime commitment. Successful people know in their youth what they want, and as they age, believe me, they still know what they want. They are willing to pay the price to become successful.

Takeaway #44
Vision

Vision means being able to see, right? I mean someone with physical 20/20 vision has perfect vision, right? Someone like me, who has physically uncorrected 20/600 vision, obviously needs glasses or contacts-possibly surgery- to obtain perfect vision, right? Some people have no physical vision at all, right?

So, I am guessing that we could come to the conclusion that some sort of physical vision, or the lack of, is something that everybody possesses, right? I guess so.

Let's talk about another type of vision—not the type of vision through the eyes, but vision through the heart, mind, and spirit. It's the type of vision in which you can close your eyes and see as clearly in your mind as watching a movie on a screen. That is the type of vision I am referring to now.

Almost every successful player, coach, business person (just name the job) is a great visualizer. This means they can see in their mind what they want and how they are going to get it. I had never heard of visualization, but even when I was a kid playing ball I would think about and dream about an upcoming game and how I would react in certain situations. I even dreamed of our team creating plays.

Believe it or not, many times the exact same plays would unfold just as I had thought and dreamed of them happening. It was as if I had already played the game and was watching a rerun on film. You know what? I was.

I had already played the game in my mind before I ever hit the playing field. I felt it in my heart and spirit that the game would be played two times, once mentally and once physically. The last time I looked one plus one equals two!

I will guarantee you that successful people do not just haphazardly do things. There is a vision for what they themselves want to become and for what they want others around them to become. ***All details are covered. There are no small details.*** There may be some changes required along the way, but the vision doesn't really change.

It's really pretty simple. All of us have the capacity to see, be it physically, mentally, or hopefully a combination of both. Vision is critical for success in whatever you are trying to accomplish. Take the God given talents that you have been created with and visualize through your mind, heart, and spirit. Challenge yourself to be great. Develop your vision for you.

Takeaway #45
Perspective of a Bird

You are probably thinking this guy's gone nuts. He's talking about birds. I can't disagree with you on one part of the last sentence in that I am gonna talk about a bird. You still may think I am nuts, but that's your opinion. And, as I've said before, that's okay because all are entitled to an opinion. So, here we go.

March 17, 2017 was my fifty-ninth birthday. My wife and me, one of my older brothers and his wife, her sister, and my nephew celebrated by going on the adventure of a lifetime—a catamaran trip in the British Virgin Islands. As I was preparing this book later that summer, the islands were devastated by Hurricane Irma. My wife and I were also devastated watching the horrific coverage of that natural disaster.

Fortunately, we will always have very vivid memories of this most beautiful of all God's creations. *The passage below is what I had written shortly after our return earlier in the spring.*

Oh, man! The pictures on television and what you have probably seen on the screen don't do these islands justice. You can truly see and feel the greatness of God when you lay eyes upon the picturesque beauty of this place. The water, islands, sea and land creatures, people and culture are all truly something to behold.

Now, my nephew was the captain of our catamaran, and he led us from island to island, showing us places that most don't get the chance to visit. We smoothly sailed the Caribbean Sea and roamed the British Virgin Islands for seven days. We were basically mesmerized and awestruck by what we saw and did.

So, I know you are probably thinking, 'What about the bird?' Here's *the what* about the bird; it is *the perspective* of a bird. One morning, we had just sailed into a beautiful harbor and moored the boat to go snorkeling. I stayed on the boat while everyone else snorkeled.

It wasn't long before I noticed some birds flying near shore and dive bombing into the sea. They were fishing, so I focused my attention on one bird and watched him for thirty or more minutes. I started wondering about perspective. Here's what I came up with.

My perspective came from sitting on a catamaran in the stunningly beautiful British Virgin Islands looking at one of God's creatures soar gracefully through the air, basically performing aerial gymnastics for me.

The bird's perspective seemed to be that it was soaring above the sea, not to put on a show for me, but to do something basic to us all—eat. That bird was dive bomb fishing and couldn't afford to miss. A miss meant no eats. You know what? That bird sure was hungry because it dive bombed a lot!

The fish's perspective, I guess, was that it was out doing its fish thing and, *bam*, it became bird food. Now, I really don't know if the bird caught every fish, but it seemed pretty accurate to me. Let me put it like this. I wish my quarterbacks were as accurate as that bird was on those fish! I watched for a long time, and then it hit me.

It's all about perspective in everything you do. From 'my perspective,' I was doing the ultimate relaxing—just kicked back and watching one of God's creatures perform aerial magic. From 'the bird's perspective,' it wasn't about performing for me; it was about fulfilling a basic need—eating. From 'the fish's perspective,' well, it was about survival.

It's really pretty simple. After I witnessed all of this, my perspective on things changed some. Through watching the bird and the fish, and thinking about what I felt about each one's perspective, it caused me to reevaluate my own perspective. In that moment, I witnessed just how precious life really is, and that I have God to thank for life.

Just think about it—a man's perspective changed by the perspective of a bird.

Takeaway #46
Don't Beat Yourself

There is an old axiom used by football coaches all across the country at every level of the sport that is great advice and just plain ol' common sense. The axiom is '***Don't beat yourself***.' The statement simply means don't do things to yourself that will cause you to lose. Plainer than that is 'Don't be dumb.' That's right. I said it, dumb.

Now, you are probably saying to yourself in a sarcastic tone, *'No joke, what a genius idea.'* Well, in reality, it is a genius idea.

In the game of football, turnovers, penalties, and mental errors made by your team will get you beat almost every time. These are all things that can be and should be avoided. More times than not, you wind up **'beating yourself.'**

Think about how that can happen in your personal life. I would bet most of the time you make mistakes that could have easily been avoided, but instead you made them anyway. **'You beat yourself.'**

We have all done that. The trick is to limit the mistakes, and **'Don't be dumb.'**

That's right, I said it again—**dumb**. If your feelings are hurt, well, that's easily fixed; don't be dumb. We've all been dumb with some decisions in our lives and wound up 'beating ourselves.' Hopefully, we learned from those dumb decisions and moved on.

The dumbest thing you can do is to keep making the same mistakes over and over instead of learning from our mistakes in the first place.

It's really pretty simple. Use common sense in all that you do. Don't be dumb in your decision making, and don't beat yourself.

Takeaway #47
Consequences

I can't speak for you, but I certainly can for me. I always want to know the consequences that may be involved before I do something. Now, to me, the word **consequence** doesn't have a big elaborate definition. It simply means what happens when you do or don't do something.

Last time I looked, I live in the greatest nation on the planet, the United States of America. Now, in this great country a person can do anything they want to do. You are probably saying, *'No you can't.'* You may be saying to yourself, *'You can't rob a bank in the United States or just haul off and punch someone in the face.'*

Stop and think about it for a minute. **Sure, you can, but after you do you will deal with the consequences of your actions.** In this country we have something called laws which dole out the consequences. We can play this game all day, but I bet you get the picture.

I will say this about consequences; they come with every action a person does or doesn't do. **Consequences are negative and positive.** I personally believe when most people hear the word consequences their first thought is negative. But think about it, if consequences are a result of our actions then they can also truly be positive.

In the athletic world, when a player works out with intensity, purpose, and passion, the consequences will be a bigger, faster, and stronger athlete. Sounds pretty positive to me. When a person truly gives their best effort in whatever they are doing usually good things happen. Sounds pretty positive to me.

Well, on the flip side, if a person is lazy and expects everything to be given to them, usually they are just 'flat out of luck.' Sounds pretty negative to me. Personally, I would rather work on the

'positive than negative.' Ultimately, it comes down to you and your choices.
Sound familiar?

Again, I can't speak for you but I can for me, and this is how I approach **'consequences.'** I live by this philosophy when it comes to how I spend my time.

'All negative people, stay away from me. I don't want any of that negative stuff you got infecting me. All you positive people, come hang around me. I want that positive stuff you got infecting me.'

It's really pretty simple. There are consequences in everything that we do. Those consequences are either 'positive or negative' dependent upon the choices we make. Hopefully, your choices will bring positive, not negative, consequences. Let's face it. We're all human and make mistakes, so hopefully you will learn from the negative as well as the positive. One thing I am sure about, we all will have to deal with consequences—positive or negative.

Takeaway #48
Life—Love it... You're Gonna Leave It

You know something I used to be really guilty of doing? I was guilty of taking life for granted. I used to just get up in the morning and go do my thing. That seemed to work for me for years, but after spending some time every year in a hospital from 2011 to 2017 due to heart or head related health issues my thought process changed. You would think that after my first visit to the hospital in 2011 I would have changed. But I will admit, I am pretty hard headed.

I guess when you are a kid **'taking life for granted'** is pretty normal because you just go about doing your kid stuff. You play, you have fun, and you're being a kid, not really thinking about a whole lot except just being a kid. Actually, the more I think about it the better that really sounds!

My brothers and I had what I would call a different type of 'kidhood'—that's childhood for you who may have not understood the term. This was our 'kidhood' experience. We would get up in the summertime and feed, saddle, and ride horses. Then, we would go and work cattle just like they did in the Old West. My daddy, Kid Marley, ran horse and cattle operations for people, which meant my brothers and I, along with others, were the ranch hands.

That was fun stuff, just like in the movies! Except in the movies they don't show you hauling hay in the blistering heat or digging post holes with hand-held tools so you can string up some barb wired fence!

They don't show it to you because it isn't fun stuff until you are finished. Anyway, there is always some good and bad in anything you do. That work made us physically, mentally, and emotionally tough, and we didn't even know it! We were kids, living our 'kidhood'.

Now, just like everyone else, we went back to school in the fall, winter and spring. Some of us played ball, joined the school band, maybe even rodeoed. Well, not to brag, but we were all good at what we did in those 'extracurricular activities'. Now, when it came to actual book learning, some of us had a little harder time than others. *I* was the *us*. My brothers were the others. You know what though? We grew throughout school. We had fun; we loved whatever we did. **We loved living from what I could tell.**

As my brothers and I grew, and individually went our separate ways to college and beyond, I noticed something that seemed not to change. We loved living. We eventually grew up, became adults, and did, and are still doing, the adult thing. **We still seem to have one commonality—our mutual love for living**. Now, how cool is that!

I really don't remember a whole lot of whining, complaining, or just plain ol' negativity. That's not to say everything was always picture perfect and times never got hard. Things did get tough, and hard, at times. But I really don't remember it affecting us in any way that took away our love for living.

Now, as an older adult with a lot of experience under my belt, I have experienced marriages, divorce, births of children, and deaths of family and friends. I can truly look back today and see how blessed we all have been. We have had great lives! I know I have had a great life and look forward to every day of it.

It's really pretty simple. We didn't bring anything into this world when we arrived and we aren't gonna take anything with us when we leave. The way we approach life, positively or negatively, has great bearing upon how we will live our life. I truly believe that you and the people you surround yourself with are the main determinate in whether or not you and those

around you live a happy life or not, so I can't emphasize this statement enough. *'Life—love it because you're gonna leave it.'*

Takeaway #49
Fountain of Youth

I would imagine almost everyone has heard of the *Fountain of Youth*. You know, it's the mythical place where you could find this type of healing water guaranteed to make you youthful again. You could swim in it or sprinkle yourself with it, even drink it, with the expectation that you would be youthful again.

I believe it was that Spanish explorer Ponce de Leon who became famous for searching for it a few hundred years ago. No doubt, some zillion others throughout the ages have searched for the *Fountain of Youth,* looking for that miraculous healing water. I guess the search never ends for many who want nothing else but to stop the aging process.

Here's a news flash for you. **I think I have actually found the Fountain of Youth**. That's right the ol' high school football coach found it. Now, for the first time ever, I am going to tell you the exact location of this treasure so you can tap into it as long as you live. Are you ready? Is the excitement building?

Well, the direct location of the *Fountain of Youth* is actually in your mind. That's right. **You possess the *Fountain of Youth* and always have possessed it.** For all of these years, people have been searching for something they already had! Think about it. *You possess the greatest computer ever created and that's your mind.* Well, wouldn't you agree that as long as you keep your computer updated, running smoothly, and keep the main parts in good working order then you have found the *Fountain of Youth*.

So, the way I see it, if we keep our mind and body active and in good working order then we have found the Fountain of Youth. Now, let's face the fact that we will all age. Just because we age doesn't mean we have to just give up. Hey, an active mind and life means a better mind and life. An inactive mind and life, well, to me, is just quitting.

My grandmother lived to be one-hundred, and she was active and sharp as a tack. She used to always say *'stay active.'* I have seen many older individuals who look and act a lot younger than they really are because they choose to stay active. They knew the *Fountain of Youth* is in the mind. I have also seen people in their forties and fifties who seem to be a lot older than they really are because of inactivity, basically giving up. I personally just don't get the giving up mentality; nor do I care to get it.

It's amazing that we possess the world's greatest computer ever built—our mind. It is totally up to all of us how we use it. **To be active or inactive is a choice each of us has to make**. One thing is for sure, we truly do know the exact location of the *Fountain of Youth*. Don't be like so many in the past and miss out on something we all possess but hardly ever tap into. Claim your *Fountain of Youth*.

It's really pretty simple. If you are searching for the *Fountain of Youth*, but you choose to stay inactive in mind and body, you will become old and worn out before your time. The flip side is also simple. If you realize you already possess the *Fountain of Youth* in your mind, then a fun active life awaits you.

Takeaway #50
Compact Players

I don't know about you, but whenever I hear the word **compact** I immediately think in terms of closeness—not tightness. In the football world, we use the word **compact** a lot. For example, we teach a quarterback to be **compact** in his throwing motion. We teach defensive linemen to be **compact** in their 'swim move technique'. Coaches also teach offensive linemen to be **compact** with their initial hand-punching technique. The list goes on and on.

Notice, I never mention the word **tight** only **compact**; the reason being—anyone who is **tight** will become **'rigid and stiff.'** **'Rigid and stiff' is not good, but 'compact and loose' is good.** Being compact is a basic requirement to becoming a good football player, but it does not come naturally. Being compact is a skill that can be improved upon with consistent daily hard work.

So, you are probably saying to yourself, *'I don't play football so what does* **compact** *have to do with me?'* Well, I really don't know; I can only give you a *guesstimation!*

I would bet that whatever you do in your job requires some sort of closeness and organization, whether it's with people, materials or logistics. I would bet if you work to become **compact, not tight** at your job, you will have fun and be more productive. I would also bet that not being rigid or stiff at work would be awesome for you and those around you. And most of all, I would bet that being **compact** at work will basically make your day go better. In turn, it will even help those around you have a better day and on and on.

Hey, just so you know, **football players who play compact are usually really good players!** I'll bet people in other professions, those who are **compact** are really good at what they do also. As a matter of fact, I'll bet—no, strike that—I *know* people who live a *compact* life are, in general, really happy people. I know that because I am one of those *compact* people!

It's really pretty simple. Tight, rigid, and stiff just isn't a comfortable way to play, conduct business, or live life. If you ask this football coach, I am going with what I know works and will make me successful, and that's *compact*.

Takeaway #51
Dependability

There is an old saying in the football coaching business, **the most important ability is dependability.** Now, think about that statement for a little bit. It's not talking about great speed, agility, strength or size. Don't get me wrong. In the game of football those are great player attributes! But what good are all those great attributes if they belong to an undependable person. Well, I can tell you the answer —*not much good.* I can't emphasize this statement enough. **You can't depend on undependable people regardless of their talent level!**

Let's define dependable. To me, it is more than a sentence; it's a way of living. So, here we go. A dependable person is one who will show up, show up on time, and give a great effort in all things every time. These are people who work to improve their individual talents every time. They put team above self by being a great teammate. In the process, they treat others with dignity and respect, all the while representing themselves, their family and organization with class everywhere they go—on and away from the playing field. Now to me, that is dependable.

As you may have noticed, I have included two seemingly simple things in my definition. **Show up and show up on time.** You may be asking yourself, '*Why both?*' Well, it's simple; they are two different things. **Show up** means just what it says. **Will people actually show up in the first place?** You may be surprised to know that a lot of times people simply don't show up for work or whatever activity they are involved in.

Also, even if they physically **show up,** they aren't mentally prepared for the task at hand. It's as if they didn't show up at all. They are simply not focused and sometimes not interested in the task at hand.

Show up on time means just that. There are many people who are always late and never on time. Neither of those undependable traits should be tolerated. In fact, they should be dealt with immediately.

Now, you handle the situation however you want, but my suggestion would be to warn the first time, punish the second time, and terminate the third time. You may even need to go from warn to terminate, depending on the situation.

You will have a chance of winning with a group of dependable people. You have no chance of winning with a group of undependable people! So, let's face a reality of the real world. **Winning and losing matters in every profession.** Unless you live on another planet, I would highly suggest that all involved in a team or organization know the exact definition of dependable from the very start.

When you get with a group of dependable people your chances of success go up immensely! It's fun to work with dependable people because you know they will be there working right alongside you and will do their best to be their best, which in turn makes everyone involved be their best. Again, notice I didn't mention talent level, or any of those great attributes we all want in a player.

Now, when you get with a group of dependable people with a lot of talent then look out because the barn door is going to get blown off its hinges. For all of you city folks, that means great things will happen!

It's really pretty simple. You can't depend on undependable people regardless of their talent level, so get rid of them. Do everything possible to surround yourself with dependable people. Your team and your organization will be much better in the long run!

Takeaway #52
Great Finisher

Let me ask you a question. If you start something, any project or task, then there has to be a finish to that something, right? You may say, yes; or, you may say, no, not necessarily. The latter answer could be because you might have to stop in the middle of that something.

To me, it's pretty simple. **When you start something, there will always be a finish.** If you stop in the middle of a project, you did finish, just not very well. So, to me, there is a start and finish to everything. **It is how you finish, that is up to you.**

In the football world, we as coaches are always looking for guys who will finish. Coaches are looking for finishers. Let me be more specific —coaches are looking for 100 percent finishers.

I watched part of an NFL *Pro Day* workout on TV a while back. This particular segment was specifically designed for defensive linemen. An NFL coach was taking three defensive linemen through drills for fifteen minutes. These drills were *ultra intense*. Hey, these guys were auditioning for a job.

I couldn't help but observe that one of the players was a better finisher than the other two. He didn't slow down as the drills got harder or more physically intense. This player was going as fast or faster at the end of every drill as he was at the beginning of every drill. The TV commentators often compared his **'finishing'** to the **'lack of finishing'** shown by the other players. They commented on the finisher's obvious mental toughness and how it allowed him to become a **'great finisher.'**

Now, at these *Pro Day* events, several NFL teams are represented. During this segment, I watched as one person was seen as a finisher while the other two players weren't viewed as finishers. NFL teams are looking for great finishers. Think about it. What organization in any field isn't? Everybody wants great finishers on their team and in their organization.

I remember when I was a little kid, my mama and daddy, as well as my grandparents, always told me to finish what I started. Now, as I grew older, I realized anyone can be a finisher, but not all can be great finishers. I would advise you the same way my parents and grandparents advised me:

If you start something, you are gonna finish, one way or another! The way you finish is totally up to you, and it is completely a reflection upon you.

It's really pretty simple. We all start something and finish something every day. It's our choice, and only our choice, how we will finish. Don't just finish—be a great finisher!

About the Author

In *Game Ready, 52 Takeaways for Winning*, author and football coach Mickey Marley, reveals the keys to cultivating talent, instilling teamwork, and creating a clear path to victory.

Sports came naturally to Mickey Marley. He grew up alongside three brothers. When the Marley brothers weren't competing, they were immersed in the physical work of their father's horse and cattle operations. "My daddy was a real-life cowboy," Coach Marley says of his late father Kid Marley. High stakes rodeoing was a passion for the elder Marley, but he made his living managing farms in Williamson County with the help of his sons.

In his youth, Coach Marley was always expected to tackle chores in the field first. High school coaches tapped into his intensity, energy and focus. Naturally, he found his voice in competition on the football field, becoming a standout athlete and collegiate player. His career decision to coach young people, first at University of Tennessee at Martin then at University School of Jackson, garnered him acclaim among players and coaches.

In this clear and concise book, Coach Marley instructively shares what he has learned from thirty-seven years of coaching, mentoring, and teaching. He resides in Jackson, Tennessee with his wife, Lisa, an educator. When not coaching football, Coach Marley enjoys spending time with his children and grandchildren, sharing their passion for sports.